21105763P

This book is to be returned on or before
the last date stamped below.   SC

10 JUN 199   LORNSHILL
               ACADEMY

D0810016

1.	5.	
2.	6.	
3.	7.	
4.	8.	

The Life of Saint Andrew: Apostle, Saint and Enigma

Stewart Lamont

Hodder & Stoughton
LONDON   SYDNEY   AUCKLAND

British Library Cataloguing in Publication Data
A record for this book is available from the British Library

ISBN 0 340 67857 7

Typeset by Avon Dataset Ltd, Bidford-on-Avon, Warks

Printed and bound in Great Britain by
Cox & Wyman Ltd, Reading, Berks

Hodder and Stoughton
A division of Hodder Headline PLC
338 Euston Road
London NW1 3BH

922.22

21105763P

PS 3/99

For Larisa

Contents

Foreword

Noah's Ark, the Ark of the Covenant, the Holy Grail are all religious artefacts that have caught the imagination. They have inspired treasure hunts and myth-making on a grand scale. Less famous and less influential in historical terms, but no less fascinating as a religious mystery, are the bones of St Andrew.

This book sets out to put flesh on the bones and to rediscover the man who was selected by Jesus to be his first disciple but who finds little place in the Gospels. It traces the legends that give Andrew a special role in the development of the Orthodox Church in both Russia and Greece, the special veneration he enjoyed in Roman Catholicism as Peter's elder brother and his adoption as the patron saint of Scotland.

To follow the travels of Andrew (and his bones in later centuries) is to take a pilgrimage through Christian history and to gain a fascinating insight into the way in which different nations reacted to the message of Christianity. New life was breathed into the bones – and a new Andrew created in the image of each nation. Finding the truth behind the diversity of images and icons is a mystery worthy of Indiana Jones and will hopefully prove as entertaining as his adventures.

Andrew: Apostle, Saint & Enigma

Modern research and scholarship have unearthed much that is new about the Bible. The legends of Andrew have been no exception to this process, and I am grateful for the works by Peterson and Dvornik listed in the bibliography as well as for the more recent work done by Ursula Hall.

I also made use of the University of Glasgow Library and would like to express my gratitude to the Very Rev. Professor Robert Davidson, formerly of the Chair of Biblical Criticism at Glasgow, for his helpful comments on my typescript.

I could not have managed to cope with the sources for the chapter on Russia without the assistance of my wife Larisa. My gratitude is also due to Judith Longman, who happily and helpfully embraced the project on arriving at Hodder.

Finally, I want to single out my agent, Andrew Hewson of John Johnson, who as well as being an old St Andrean friend he has the special privilege of being an Andrew.

S. J. L.
July 1996

1

Andrew the Enigma

Andrew, the fisherman from Galilee, is an enigma. First to be called as a disciple, senior to his brother Peter in age and part of the core group who followed Jesus in his short ministry, Andrew slips elusively out of the Bible and disappears into the mists of legend. Hundreds of years later he surfaces, restored to a prominent place among the founders of the Christian Church, and is adopted as the patron saint of several countries.

In many ways, Andrew is an ideal patrol saint: facts are scarce and legends about him abound. No one is too particular about whether they are historically accurate, thus enabling his persona to be invoked in a variety of ways. On the other hand, his disappearance from the scene as the Christian Church struggled to establish its identity raises more questions than the reliable documents and data have ever been able to answer. Did he conduct a mission around the Black Sea area? If so, did he go north into Russia – 900 years before that country became Christian – or did he turn back, creating the first bishop of Constantinople and thus founding the apostolic line of the Orthodox Church? Did he then meet his death in Patras in south-western Greece, martyred on an X-shaped cross by a Roman ruler whose wife had been converted by the apostle?

The mysteries do not end after Andrew's death. Mark Antony's famous funeral oration for Caesar in which he claimed, 'The evil that men do lives after them, the good is oft interred with their bones', is not true of Andrew. Long after his death, Andrew's bones have been used for good causes. Divided into lots, swapped, revered and claimed to be the source of miracles, some have disappeared and others survive as the focus of devotion for Roman Catholics in various places. One is tempted to add that if all the bones of Andrew which were being revered in various sites at one particular time in history had been brought together, the Church might have had two apostles for the price of one. They would each have had a job.

In the medieval era, when the veneration of relics was at its height, there were two Churches, both claiming apostolic supremacy – the Roman or Western Church and the Orthodox or Eastern one. Orthodoxy may have gone marching on in the belief that Andrew had founded its patriarchate, but Andrew's body was not mouldering in any grave. In the Western Church popes and bishops were moving his bones around proudly, contradicting any idea that Andrew was the property of the Eastern Church. This renewed interest on the part of both halves of Christendom had the positive effect of establishing a new reputation for Peter's elder brother.

In Scotland Andrew was to become the focus of national aspiration. The little town on the east coast named after the apostle (St Andrews) quickly grew into a powerful ecclesiastical centre that would promote that ambition. The legend of Regulus (abbot and saint, depending on which version you choose), who had a vision that the bones that resided in Patras should be saved and brought to Scotland, tells how the apostle's bones came directly by sea to St Andrews. This conveniently established a direct link between Scotland and the place in which Andrew was martyred, ignoring the claims of the places in Italy which harboured relics. But, most significant of all, it omitted to mention the alternative version of how Andrew's bones arrived in St Andrews – that they were brought there from Hexham in England. The embarrassing fact that Scotland's patron saint, whose symbol was carried into battle by Scottish armies repelling English invaders, might actually have been a gift from the Old Enemy would not exactly have been good propaganda.

Did St Regulus really exist? Where are the bones which once reposed in the grandeur of St Andrews cathedral? Did Andrew really die at Patras? Or, more fundamentally, did Andrew really travel anywhere after his return to Galilee following the death of Jesus? These are just a few of the questions surrounding the enigma of Andrew that this book will set out to address, albeit in the knowledge that there is no final, undisputed answer to any of them.

Perhaps that is how Andrew would have wanted it. His scant appearances in the Scriptures reveal his character as modest and retiring, content to take a back seat and be an enabler (bringing others to Jesus or assisting with the feeding of the five thousand). We are left by the Gospel writers in no doubt about the fiery character of some of his fellow fishermen-disciples (e.g., the sons of Zebedee, James and John, who were nicknamed Boanerges, 'sons of thunder', by Jesus). His brother Peter seems to have been a blend of bluster and bullishness charging off in pursuit of his passions, while his older, steadier brother receded more and more into the background.

Homily writers (and some biographers of St Andrew) have exploited the few acorns of information in the Gospels and have nurtured great oaks that attempt to place Andrew close to the heart of the Christian faith. I have no quarrel with this legitimate enterprise. The stories of the saints were written to

3

inspire those who hear them. Even relics provide a tangible link with the holy person and with the place in which they are exhibited. We should not be too quick to condemn fabulous stories about saints or the wish to have some kind of physical reminder of a great figure from the past.

Those who feel repelled by the veneration of relics may look upon such practices with a sense of superiority. Yet in our own time the belongings of famous people can fetch huge sums of money simply because of their aura. At its worst it is a kind of idolatry, but those who think it harmless to collect Elvis Presley's jumpsuit or Winston Churchill's cigar butts perhaps have an insight into the simple faith of those who treated the saints of the Church as spiritual heroes and treasured their relics. As time went by, the place in which the hallowed object was exhibited became hallowed itself and it almost ceased to matter if the object was genuine. This is what has happened with the Shroud of Turin (shown recently to date from the period in the Middle Ages when relic veneration was at its height). While acknowledging the counterfeit nature of the cloth, the Pope still feels happy to commend it to Catholics as a catalyst for faith in the Resurrection.

As for the fabulous nature of many of the Andrew legends, we cannot afford to be too disdainful towards these either. It was the custom, before books replaced oral history, to tell stories about famous heroes that recounted the kinds of action consistent with their character or status. Come to think of it, there is nothing alien to our own age about this. We now accept (after some pious reluctance earlier this century) the idea of portraying Christ on film, television or in musicals such as *Godspell*. (It is regarded as legitimate piety.) We can appreciate Shakespeare's versions of Macbeth or Richard III, knowing that his portrayal of these characters is at variance with known facts. (We call it dramatic licence.) The fictitious Sherlock Holmes and James Bond became so popular that when the authors' original corpus had been exhausted, new scenarios were created involving these characters (imitation being the sincerest form of flattery). Much the same happened with Andrew in the early Church. A combination of dramatisation, fictionalisation and imitation resulted in Gospels being created that featured biblical characters and incidents.

This 'apocryphal' literature often had another, hidden, agenda. It was designed to promote a particular school of theology. The period AD 150–350 was particularly rife with disputes, splits and rivalries between various groups and centres in the early Church. After Rome crushed the Jewish revolt in AD 70 and rased Jerusalem, the focus of activity in the early Church switched to cities such as Alexandria, Antioch and Rome, which developed their own 'spin' on the Gospel. As well as this geographical divergence, there was a theological diversity. This gave rise to a healthy debate – and some theologies that were judged to be distinctly unhealthy, akin to falling victim to a nasty disease. The main heresies held that salvation was a question of knowing certain hidden truths (Gnosticism); that the world was a battle-ground between good and evil (Manicheanism); that since God could be put to death, Jesus must only have *seemed* to be a man (Docetism); and that he was wholly human (Arianism).

The apocryphal literature featuring Andrew, as we shall see in chapter 3, is coloured by these factors. Alas, as literature it is not very good. One of the least credible tales is the *Pistis Sophia*, which dates from the second half of the third century. Originally written in Greek, it survives only in Coptic but adopts a style common to the Byzantine world in which the hero (here the post-Resurrection Jesus) is asked questions:

> Andrew stepped up and spoke, 'My Lord, concerning
> the solution of the sixth repentance of the Pistis Sophia,
> thy enlightening power first prophesied through David
> in the 129th Psalm wherein the Power said' [he then
> quotes verses 3–8].
>
> Jesus answers, 'Well, Andrew, you blessed one, this is
> the solution of the repentance. Amen, amen I say to you,
> I will perfect you in all mysteries of light, and in all *gnosis*
> from the Inner of the Inner to the Outer of the Outer.'

It doesn't take much forensic skill to see this for what it was –
pure Gnosticism – and that it is somewhat out of tune with the
Jesus we meet in the conventional Gospels.

Gradually, an accepted canon was established as central and
the more outlandish literature (in style or theology) was margin-
alised. This is what happened to the Acts of Andrew, the Acts
of Andrew and Matthias and the Acts of Peter and Andrew. All
three developed differently in their various versions in Syriac,
Coptic, Greek and Latin, circulating in different geographical
areas. For instance, the Coptic version of a story that is
generally agreed to have taken place in the Black Sea area has
Andrew encountering a couple of sphinxes – clearly playing
to the local audience!

All three of these books of Acts were subject to editing and
reissue in later centuries (as happened when Gregory of Tours
revised the Andrew legends in the early medieval period). Since
the Reformation they have languished, available only in scholarly translations which tend to underline the awkward and
incredible storylines. The Acts of Andrew and Matthias had

never been translated from the original Greek until 1958, when Peter Peterson included it in his study of the growth of the Andrew legends. Rather than omit these important sources of 'Andreana' from this book, but conscious that they are less than thrilling to read in their original form, I have opted to summarise and paraphrase, thus making available, for the first time in popular form, the full Andrew legends. I hope readers will forgive a sense of fun intruding from time to time and not take this for impiety.

Another facet of this book is my intention to cover the subject from a historical perspective of two thousand years. This may seem odd, since it is a biography, a life of a man who died at the very latest around AD 70. My reason is that there is not one Andrew but several, who emerge at various stages of history; the apostle seems to have enjoyed a wonderful capacity for being reinvented.

The scholarly consensus seems to be that there are cycles in the development of the Andrew legends. The fact that no tradition exists about him in the early Church puts some distance between the Galilean fisherman (chapter 2) and the later character of the various Acts, all of which had made an appearance by AD 500 (chapter 3). The Western cult of Andrew was given a boost by the influence of two Gregorys, one being the aforementioned Bishop of Tours (died AD 594), who edited his own version of two of the legends, the other being Pope Gregory the Great (died AD 604), who gave Andrew a prominent place in Rome and Catholicism (chapter 6). Yet another stage in the cycle occurred in the ninth century, when attempts were made by Greek Orthodox churchmen to set up Andrew as a kind of anti-Peter to boost the status of Constantinople (chapter 4). I have been able (by virtue of translations made for me by my Russian wife) to include a chapter on the role of Andrew as patron saint of Russia (chapter 5). The complicated tale of how Andrew acquired the status of patron saint in Scotland is contained in chapter 8. I finish with reflections on Andrew and the contemporary Scottish psyche (chapter 9).

The fact that there is renewed interest in St Andrew in Scotland is, I hope, a positive development. It is said that St Andrew's Day dinners may soon be more popular among Scots expatriates than that other annual saturnalia of haggis and hagiolatry, the Burns Supper. Those who are worried that not enough is known about the Andrew in whose honour the celebration takes place need have no fear. For two hundred years this handicap has scarcely worried the Burnsians, who have been able to enjoy the Bard in contradictory roles as both proletarian and poseur, lecher and moralist!

In researching the book I came across a reference taken from the *Scottish American Journal* of 1884 of 'Scotch dishes for St Andrew's Day'. The recipe for 'Hotch-potch' is accompanied by a jokey little poem which describes that there are 'carrots intill't, beef intill't, and turnip intill't' (and so it goes on). I know a corny (but true) story based on the poem. A person unfamiliar with the Scots tongue innocently asked, 'Yes, but what's intill't?' (Scots for 'into it'). The cook to whom she addressed the question replied by repeating the poem, after which the same question inevitably came, followed by the repetition of the poem, *ad nauseam*. I hope that this book will not prove too much of a hotch-potch based on bones, or repetitious, and that at the end of it the reader will agree that the story of Andrew has more intill't than a pious legend.

2

Andrew the Disciple

The first curious thing about Andrew is his name. A Jew by birth and upbringing, he has a Greek name. Andreas is entirely Greek in origin. It can be found as early as Herodotus (485–425 BC) and means 'manly'. The fact that a number of the Galilean group who became Jesus's inner core of disciples had Greek names (e.g., Peter and Philip) derives from the cultural background of Galilee. It was Hellenistic as well as Jewish.

Galilee has been called the 'fifth Gospel' because its people, its society and its geography were so central to the message of Jesus of Nazareth, whose own home was a short journey from the shores of the Sea of Galilee (or Gennaseret, as it was also known). For that reason it is worth making a swift summary of the history and culture of the region.

A thousand years before the Christian era, Galilee had been part of a Jewish state in the golden time of David and Solomon. The northern part of that kingdom had always been subject to foreign influences, and David had managed to paper over the cracks in creating a unified kingdom. As soon as Solomon, his son, was dead the northerners went their own way and the kingdom was split into Judah in the south (centred on Jerusalem) and Israel in the north. Both – as the Old Testament relates – fell prey to the great empires of the Middle East,

Assyria and Babylonia. Galilee was then annexed by the Persian empire until the rise of Alexander the Great, who by the time of his death at the age of thirty-three in 323 BC had created an empire which stretched from the Aegean Sea in the west to the Indus River in the east, and from the Danube River in the north to the Sahara Desert in the south. His zeal to create a civilisation based on Hellenistic culture inevitably found resistance in the conquered lands, but resulted in the international acceptance of the Greek language.

Alexander's empire was split by his successors into three areas. The Seleucids of Syria ruled the area around Galilee. Although Jewish nationalism flared in the second century BC, when the Hasmonaean (Maccabbean) revolt took place, the Hellenistic period of history lasted until 31 BC, when Augustus incorporated the last of Alexander's former kingdom into the Roman empire. In the previous generation Pompey had brought the area under Roman reorganisation by setting up the Decapolis (a free league of cities to the east of the Jordan); and in 57 BC the provincial governor, Gabininius, divided Palestine into five administrative areas.

To combat Jewish nationalism, the Romans installed Herod the Great as a client king. After his death in 4 BC, the nucleus of the Jewish nation (centred on Jerusalem) was enrolled as a Roman province named Judea and allowed a certain amount of devolved power under a high priest and council (the Sanhedrin). To the east and north-east the territory was given to a puppet king, Herod Antipas, one of Herod's sons. His half-brother, Philip Herod, the 'Tetrarch', ruled the Transjordan area further to the north, residing in Caesarea Philippi. The territories of Herod Antipas and Philip met at the north end of the Sea of Galilee, and there was a customs post in Capernaum.

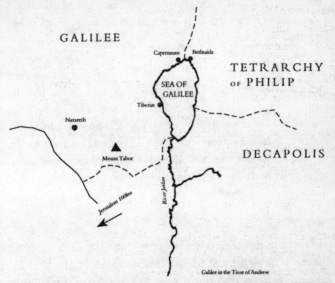

Galilee in the Time of Andrew

It therefore contained what today we would call a clerical middle class, some of whom were the 'tax gatherers' mentioned in the Gospels.

A little further along the northern end of the lake (on Philip's side of the frontier formed by the River Jordan) was the town of Bethsaida (whose name means, literally, the 'house of fish'). It was here that Andrew and his brother Peter operated their fishing business. Bethsaida, which was raised to city status by Philip, stood on one of the main trade routes with the Far East, the Via Maris, and had its posh quarter, named Julias after the daughter of Emperor Augustus.

While many parts of the Roman empire suffered from dire poverty, with a huge gap between rich and poor, the area around the north end of the lake was modestly prosperous for the locals as well as for the colonial officials and the traders. The fertile

11

land enabled wheat to be grown as well as crops of olives and figs. The sea yielded fish – a cod-like variety (which has acquired the name 'Peter's fish') – and silver sprats that presumably formed the shoals that feature in the Gospel stories. They in turn brought silver in the form of currency. Salted and exported to cities like Jerusalem or sold to the passing population, fish provided a decent living. The idea of the disciples as barefoot Huckleberry Finns, who did a little idle fishing, does not square with reality. The fact that the families of Andrew and Peter, and Zebedee's sons James and John, apparently had their own boats and hired assistants makes them nearer to being small businessmen than horny-handed sons of toil.

Today the region's biggest industry is tourism – and the visitors are not simply the pilgrims who come to view the places in which most of the Gospel incidents took place. Modern Israelis who don't want to leave Israel for holidays (and pay the penalty of being taxed if they do) can now choose from several luxury hotels in resorts on the Sea of Galilee, such as Tiberias. The city itself was built by Herod Antipas and named in honour of the Emperor Tiberias (who reigned AD 14–37). It still sports the hot-spring baths that delighted its Roman clientele and, on one occasion, me when on Christmas Day I luxuriated in the hot water of the outdoor spa, with the cool drizzle on my face, as I looked across to the green hills of the east side of the lake. However, the Jews of the time boycotted the city because it was built on the sacred site of a former graveyard and was therefore unclean. Jesus, in keeping with the radical attitude he took towards social lepers and outcasts, does not seem to have shared this inhibition (cf. John 6:1, 23 and 21:1).

Herod Antipas does not get a good press in the Gospels or the histories of the time. His first wife was the daughter of the king of Nabatea, and he forsook her for Herodias who, as well as being his half-brother's wife, seems to have been cast in the Delilah/Jezebel mould. Their relationship was incestuous, according to Jewish Levitical law (Lev. 18:16 and 20:21), and was therefore a source of scandal among his subjects. Chief among his outspoken critics was a charismatic preacher operating in and around the desert wastes to the south of the Sea of Galilee – John the Baptist.

The thrust of his message was that a new kingdom was soon to be inaugurated under God's kingship. That itself was enough to make people sit up and take notice: at long last a return to the golden era, an end to colonial rule, foreign cultural imperialism and taxation without representation. The manifesto fell on receptive ears. Nationalism lurked close to the surface among Rome's Jewish subjects, and anything that might signify the end of occupation was welcome. It also made Herod Antipas prick up his ears, since it would mean the end of his reign. If the seditious nature of John's message was not enough for Herod Antipas, the other part of his teaching was even less designed to curry favour with the prince. John advocated that those who did not repent of their sins and become (through the once-and-for-all act of baptism) utterly changed persons would not participate in this kingdom. No doubt Herod was indifferent to the theological thrust of this message, which implied the worthlessness of a system of sacrifices and indulgences that could be used by the unscrupulous to salve their consciences or wipe the slate clean by buying pardon. However, the moral cutting edge of John's preaching encouraged people to think of Herod Antipas as a reprobate.

John the Baptist was one of a kind. Those who belong to this kind usually appear in times of decadence to challenge the flabbiness and oppressiveness of the system. They are a direct threat to the ruler, and they often pay the price. John was arrested – and thereby silenced. But Herodias wanted revenge – his head on a platter – and she got it, literally, as the incident described in Mark 6:14–29 reveals. The execution of John did not enhance Herod's popularity. Not long after, when the Nabatean king declared war on Herod to satisfy his daughter's honour and inflicted a humiliating defeat, it was widely seen as retribution by Herod's far from adoring subjects. Herod's career ended ignominiously in exile in Gaul when he tried to persuade the maniacal and dissolute emperor Caligula (AD 37–41) to make him a proper king.

Before his arrest John had baptised two people who would be central to subsequent events. The first was Jesus, who was to develop John's teaching about the kingdom of God from the promise of a future event to a reality centred on his own person. Jesus was told that he too was on the deathlist of Herod Antipas, whom he called 'that fox' (Luke 13:31), and avoided an inevitable clash by going back to his local area at the north end of the lake to begin his ministry there.

The other person whom John baptised has so far had little mention – Andrew. Despite the fact that the Gospels are sparing in their references to Jesus's first disciple, from what has been outlined so far we can begin to form a sketchy portrait of his background and the factors that shaped his life. Sherlock Holmes would have been able to tell us a great deal about Andrew before he even opened the Gospels.

Jesus – and Andrew – spoke a version of Hebrew called

14

Aramaic. (Some of the sayings of Jesus make even more sense, or develop rhythm or rhyme, when they are translated back into this tongue, which has, I am told, much the same relationship to ancient Hebrew as Scots has to English.) As a Galilean, Andrew's accent would have been as distinctive as that of his brother, Peter, whose manner of speech gave him away as he waited in the courtyard while Jesus was on trial before the Sanhedrin (Matthew 26:73).

However, we should not conclude that Andrew would have lacked knowledge of other languages apart from Aramaic. Although the synagogue school at Bethsaida that Andrew most probably attended would have had a curriculum limited to moral and religious content, he would have encountered in his daily life a variety of different languages. Latin-speaking agents of the Roman empire and traders passing through Bethsaida on the Via Maris (perhaps buying fish from the family business) would all have brought a cosmopolitan atmosphere to the town. Andrew inhabited a multicultural society on which Greek/Hellenistic ideas had left their stamp, not least the Greek language (with which, it is reasonable to assume, he was also familiar).

Notwithstanding Andrew's familiarity with the Gentile world, it is improbable that he was literate. Paul appears to have been the only literate one among the apostles. The fact that Andrew's brother Peter is credited with two letters written in Greek in the New Testament is neither here nor there. Most biblical scholars would agree that it is unlikely that he wrote them and that they were attributed to him as a revered leader within the early Church. This not uncommon practice was intended not to deceive but to pay homage to the fictitious author. It is not dissimilar to the practice in later centuries of attributing paintings to the 'school of Rembrandt' or of giving musical compositions the name of a prominent person (e.g., the *Brandenburg Concertos* or the *Bonaparte Symphony,* renamed the *Eroica*). We do not treat these creations as frauds or forgeries on this account and similarly have not undermined the content of the Petrine epistles by learning that they were written by anonymous authors.

As we have seen, Jewish nationalism had always been a significant factor in the area. Galilee had been a hotbed of Maccabbean revolt, and there still was wide support for the idea of throwing off the Roman yoke and going it alone, not simply among groups of rebellious fanatics. Although Jesus's teaching of the kingdom of God did not involve taking direct political action (and he suggested rendering unto Caesar whatever was the Roman emperor's due), he was inevitably seen by many as the messiah figure who might, just might, provide the longed-for deliverance. An example of a person being drawn into Jesus's circle holding such views is Simon the Zealot (as his name makes clear, a member of one group of self-styled freedom fighters).

What we must now consider is how far Andrew's own sympathies lay in this direction. The eminent biblical scholar Oscar Cullmann, in his book *Peter: Disciple, Apostle, Martyr,* draws attention to the title Jesus gives Peter in Matthew 16:17, when he calls him 'Simon Baryona'. The older writers take this to mean 'bar-Yona' which means literally 'son of Jonah'. John, in his Gospel (1:42), changes this to 'son of John' (*huios Ioannou*), which gave rise to Greek legends about the parents of Peter and Andrew, who were given the names Johannes and Johanna respectively. However, as Cullmann points out, the word *Baryona*, written without the hyphen, means 'extremist or terrorist'. Was Peter (and by implication his family) part of the patriotic front? Or did Matthew (writing in Greek from several sources) simply mix up the two Simons and tar Simon Peter with the brush of the Zealots?

John the Baptist's radical message of solidarity with the poor clearly found favour with Andrew. Amplified by Jesus, it also found favour with the heavily taxed Galileans, who laboured under the burden of three taxes – one levied by the Romans, one by the king and another by the temple authorities in Jerusalem. It was driving many smallholders into debt or ruin and creating an underclass. Such factors made the political climate heavy with the threat of insurrection.

We can never know for sure, but the subsequent actions of both Andrew and Peter were to show them to be far from satisfied with the political status quo in Palestine. As fishermen, they would be travelling around the lake, landing at locations within different provinces. Their vessel would have been the ideal vehicle for clandestine activity, out of the reach of Roman soldiers or puppet princes.

To say Andrew was a practising Jew tells us a little more about him. The style of synagogue worship in Galilee was much plainer than in the temple in Jerusalem, rather as a Welsh chapel is not like Brompton Oratory. That would have suited fishermen, whose spirituality tends to a simpler style of faith and worship. However, we can conclude that Andrew was not totally content in his faith. That was what made him such a ready convert.

Whether Andrew was first converted by John the Baptist or by Jesus depends on which Gospel you read. John's Gospel gives Andrew a position of leadership and mentions a number of incidents in which he is a key witness or an enabler. Mark makes Andrew play second fiddle to Peter. Luke and Matthew edit poor Andrew out of most incidents. Let us therefore review the incidents in the four Gospels which involve Andrew and scan them for further clues about him.

Mark (1:16–18) tells how Jesus 'passing by the Sea of Galilee, saw Simon and Andrew, Simon's brother, casting a net into the sea, for they were fishermen. And Jesus said to them, "Follow me, and I will make you fishers of men." And, immediately leaving their nets behind, they followed him.'

Mark mentions Andrew again in the list of the twelve disciples (3:16–19) and in two other incidents. The first occurs on a sabbath in the synagogue at Capernaum where Mark implies that the family of Peter and Andrew (now) live. Jesus's teaching causes a buzz and then we read (1:29–31): 'Immediately having left the synagogue, they entered the house of Simon and of Andrew, with James and John. Now Simon's mother-in-law lay fevered and immediately they told him of her. And coming, having taken her up by the hands he raised her up; and the fever left her, and she served them.'

This incident is retold by both Matthew and Luke, who as well as original material in their Gospels, base many events on Mark's account, which is generally agreed to be the earliest of the four Gospels. They sometimes polish and rearrange the word order in Mark, but in this case they retell the story of Peter's mother-in-law and edit Andrew out completely. Peter Peterson, in his book *Andrew, Brother of Simon Peter*, concludes: 'That both evangelists independently omitted Andrew's name from their rewrites of Mark shows clearly that Andrew as disciple (or for that matter as apostle) was historically a person of no importance whatsoever' (see Matt. 8:14–15, Luke 4:38–9).

The other Markan appearance of Andrew occurs in 13:3–4, when Jesus is sitting on the Mount of Olives opposite the Jerusalem temple, and James and John and Andrew ask him, 'Tell us, when will this be, and what will be the sign when these things will be accomplished?' Jesus then goes on to give an apocalyptic prediction of the destruction of Jerusalem and collapse of the existing world order.

Matthew mentions Andrew in his list of twelve disciples (10:2–4) and recounts the calling of the first ones (4:18–22), changing the word order a little but still retaining Andrew. However, as for the rest of his Gospel, all is silence.

Luke is even more dismissive. In the calling of the first disciples (5:1–11), he cuts Andrew out of the story, replacing him with James and John, the sons of Zebedee, 'Simon's partners'. Indeed, Luke (and Acts) continue this indifference, mentioning Andrew only in lists of the twelve disciples (Luke 6:12–16, Acts 1:13).

It is only in the Gospel of John that Andrew plays a significant role. The scene of the first incident takes place at Bethany beyond the Jordan, where John the Baptist was preaching (1:35–44). 'The next day John was standing with two of his disciples and looking at Jesus as he walked, he said, "Behold the lamb of God!" The two disciples heard him speaking and followed Jesus. But Jesus, having turned, saw them following him, and said, "What are you looking for?" They replied, "Rabbi (meaning teacher), where are you staying?" He said to them, "Come and see." They went then and saw where he was staying, and with them they stayed that day, for it was about the tenth hour. Andrew, Simon Peter's brother, was one of the two who heard John speak and followed him. He first found his own brother, Simon, and said to him, "We have found the Messiah" (which means anointed). He took him to Jesus. Looking at him, Jesus said, "You are Simon, son of John? [See above.] You shall be called Cephas (which means 'rock')." The next day he decided to leave for Galilee and sought out Philip. Jesus said to him, "Come and see." Now Philip was from Bethsaida, the city of Cephas and Andrew.'

This version is rather different from the one we find in Mark/ Matthew/Luke. Andrew and Peter are identified with Bethsaida, not Capernaum, and in this incident are to be found beyond the southern edge of the Sea of Galilee. Furthermore they are clearly identified as disciples of John the Baptist. These apparent contradictions can quite easily be explained. It is not beyond the bounds of possibility that the fishing boat was plying on the southern side of the lake. The brothers perhaps arranged to go to one of John's 'rallies', much as a Scot from Aberdeen might have arranged to go down to Glasgow for one of the Billy Graham crusades in Glasgow during the Fifties. There they became converted and were ready to respond eagerly to the invitation of the man whom John the Baptist identified as the Lamb of God.

As for Bethsaida/Capernaum, the two towns are close together. It is possible that John (the Gospel writer) lumped them together in error. Even more plausible is the possibility that Andrew and Peter moved from Bethsaida to Capernaum. Two reasons immediately suggest themselves for this. Either Peter married and moved nearer his wife's family home or, more simply, they went there because Capernaum was nearer to the market for their fish in the towns of Galilee and better placed to get the fish quickly to the Jerusalem market. I am tempted to add that crossing the frontier into Galilee meant avoiding the aforementioned customs post and may have been prompted by a shrewd piece of tax avoidance.

John's Gospel features Andrew in two other incidents. The famous feeding of the five thousand is carried by the other evangelists, but they omit the walk-on part assigned to Andrew (John 6:5–14) in which the disciple tells Jesus: 'There is a lad here who has five barley loaves and two fish; but what are they among so many?'

The other incident, arguably more significant, is the story of the Greeks coming to Jesus because it places Andrew in a position of influence (12:20–34): 'The Greeks went to Philip, the one from Bethsaida of Galilee, and asked him, "Sir we want to see Jesus." Philip went and told Andrew. Andrew and Philip went and told Jesus.' (Here, once again, John places Bethsaida in Galilee.)

Why does John restore Andrew to a more significant place than the others? The answer may lie partly in a piece of papyrus called the Muratorian Fragment, thought to date from the end of the second century, which credits Andrew with the commissioning of the Gospel of John. John asked his fellow disciples whether he should undertake the project. They were to fast for three days in order to seek a revelation. The tactic apparently worked, for 'On the same night it was revealed to Andrew of the apostles that John should describe in his own name all the facts and that all should review his writing.' Was this a case of John repaying the compliment by giving greater prominence to the man who got him the commission, or is the fragment an attempt to explain why he was given it?

Although Andrew was present at the Last Supper, we hear nothing of him after that from John. He is not mentioned in the list of those present at the miraculous catch of fish at the end of the Gospel, when a group of disciples led by Peter encounter the Risen Christ as they are fishing (21:1–14).

Peter goes on to play a leading role in the Church after Pentecost, and apart from Paul, the two disciples named James (the brother of Jesus, and Zebedee's son, who was put to death by Agrippa), Stephen and one or two others, no other original disciple was apparently important enough to make an impact on the early Church or on commentators such as Josephus (a Galilean Zealot who became a collaborator and historian of the turbulent events during the first century).

Where did Andrew go while Peter, bearing his keys, went back to Jerusalem, on to Joppa and eventually to Rome to found his church? It is strange that all the literature of the early years of the new movement omits Andrew, even as a close relative of Peter and one who had been a witness to the events of the Gospels. We have already seen that Andrew is conspicuous by his absence from the writings of Luke, who was writing and operating in the very area of Greece in which Andrew was destined to minister and be martyred. Nor does Paul in all his travels come across Andrew.

The mundane explanation is that Andrew was content to let his younger brother take the limelight. If that is so, our quest for Andrew should end here. However, there is another early fragment which may give us a clue to his whereabouts. Origen (*c.* AD 184–254), as quoted by Eusebius, the greatest church historian of the period, d. AD 340) states that after Pentecost the disciples drew lots for the mission fields, with 'Andrew receiving Scythia' (in modern terms, the area of southern Russia and Ukraine on the north side of the Black Sea). It is here that we next pick up traces of the elusive apostle.

3

Andrew the Apostle

If Herod and his son Antipas were bad news for the mission of Jesus, Agrippa was an even more dangerous enemy from within the Jewish people itself. He had grown up in Rome, effectively ingratiating himself with the Roman elite, and when Caligula became emperor in AD 37 he was given Herod Antipas's old kingdom to run. In AD 41 Judea, Samaria and Idumea followed, thus restoring the former kingdom of Herod the Great to one king.

Agrippa had acquired that habit of courtiers throughout the ages of running with the hare and hunting with the hounds. He represented himself to the Jews as a devout Jew, humouring the Pharisees. To the Hellenists he behaved like a Greek, undertaking grandiose building projects. To the Romans he toadied, like the quisling he was. And it was all a huge success. When required, he showed that he could be as tough as his predecessors. One of the victims of his crackdowns was James, son of Zebedee the Galilean fisherman, now a leading figure in the Christian community in Jerusalem, who was executed in AD 44. Peter fled Jerusalem to escape being next in line.

It was obvious that life was not going to be easy for the disciples in their new role as 'apostles'. James's role as leader was taken over by James, the brother of Jesus, whom Paul seems to have treated as an apostle. Paul himself, of course, had famously switched sympathies and joined the Christians (in AD 38) and quickly acquired the status of apostle. The title 'apostle' was therefore not confined to the original disciples but embraced the leadership of the emerging Church. (In Greek *apostolos* means 'one who is sent forth'.) Some argue that there were as many as seventy disciples but that twelve were highlighted in the Gospels in order to correspond symbolically with the twelve tribes of Israel. The twelve apostles were their successors, and Andrew figures among lists of apostles compiled generations later.

Peter, his brother, had assumed a leadership role but already there was tension between Peter and Paul, with Paul promoting Gentile Christian converts and Peter seeing the Church as a Jewish movement. The letter of Barnabas describes the apostles as 'ruffians of the deepest dye', and the Gospels are not exactly flattering either about the twelve, who are constantly portrayed as getting hold of the wrong end of the stick or falling short of the teaching of Jesus.

Where would Andrew have stood in all this? Would he have been content to play second fiddle to Peter, or would he have seen his impetuous brother as a poor substitute for Jesus? Did they part company, Peter staying in Jerusalem while Andrew returned to Galilee to run the family business? Of his doings in the immediate post-Pentecost period we know nothing. Acts and the letters of Paul do not mention him at all. However, the mission to Scythia which was mentioned by Origen is the subject of a book of its own, the Acts of Andrew, which supplies an answer to the question: what happened to Andrew? Whether we can rely on its veracity is another matter.

The Acts of Andrew is not the only work to feature the adventures of our hero. It was probably the first to chronicle his exploits and had a decidedly Gnostic flavour to it, which accounts for the fact that Pope Gelasius (AD 492–6) placed it in the 'unacceptable' category when compiling a list of books that the faithful might or might not read. Nor is the Acts of Andrew a single work. New stories and legends seem to have been added and different versions of this and other works were in circulation in the different language/culture zones of the early Christian Church – Greek, Syriac, Coptic and Latin.

In the next chapter we will see that many of these stories overlap or are derivative versions of the same story. Before we do a little detective work on these, exploring why and when they were written – and by whom – it is worth looking at what they contain. Those expecting something very similar to the New Testament will be disappointed and will begin, perhaps, to sympathise with Pope Gelasius. Although written from pious motives and containing allusions to biblical incidents, the Andrew who emerges is far from the tight-lipped bit player of the canonical Gospels. Here we find storylines akin to the plots of grand opera and a hero more like Baron Münchhausen or Don Quixote, an adventurer who slays dragons, banishes demons and rescues women from the lusts of the flesh. Enter, Andrew – the superhero.

The first of our legends is a Byzantine text called the Narratio, which incorporates material from several sources. It begins with Andrew crossing 'like a falling star' from east to west. Leaving Bithynia, he entered Nicaea (scene in AD 325 of the conference to hammer out a creed that would exclude the followers of Arius, who taught that Jesus was not God). The east gate of the city was haunted by evil spirits who ambushed travellers, and Andrew exorcised the place, making it safe for visitors.

The Near East in the Time of Andrew

Sailing for Scythia, he came to Sevastapol and the Crimea, where he evangelised, before returning to Sinope on the southern coast of the Black Sea (modern Turkey). At the beginning of the Christian era Sinope was the most important trading centre between Asia Minor, Parthia and the north. Under the king of Pontus, Mithridates, a century previously it had acquired strategic importance, which it still retained. Constantinople had yet to eclipse it as pre-eminent port of the region.

Andrew's reason for visiting Sinope was to rescue the apostle Matthias, who was in prison with other Christians. Killing the guards 'by prayer', Andrew opened the doors of the prison and rescued Matthias. Before they could make their escape, however, the savage inhabitants seized Andrew, tortured him and threw him into prison. The apostle laid hands on the statue of a man and told it, 'Fear the sign of the cross and pour water on these harsh people until they turn to the true God.' A huge jet of water soared higher and higher from the statue and the trembling populace begged Andrew to relent. He stopped the jet, walked free from prison and began to preach to the people, baptising many and founding a church before sailing off along the coast towards Byzantium (Constantinople).

Settling in Argyropolis (Silver City), a suburb of Byzantium, he founded a church and laid hands on Stachys, who is described as one of the seventy disciples, and ordained him as Bishop of Byzantium. The prevailing godlessness of the people and cruelty of the ruler Zeuxippos persuaded him to leave and go west. (This incident is regarded by most scholars as a forgery inserted in the text in a later era to bolster the claims of the apostolic foundation of Byzantium: see next chapter.)

Continuing through Thessalonia and Greece, Andrew went south-west to Achaea, arriving in the city of Patras. He was successful in persuading the people to reject 'Hellenism's darkness' for the 'bath of immortality' and to be 'born again through God's baptism'. Among his converts was Maximilla, wife of the proconsul Aegeates, a man of 'cruel and bestial temper'. Andrew persuaded her to spit on the Greek gods and, together with her relative Ephidamia, she became a Christian and gave up sleeping with her husband. Enraged, Aegeates had Andrew thrown into prison and threatened to have him tortured. Maximilla visited Andrew in prison, where he continued prophesying hell and damnation for Aegeates and those who clung to things 'as transitory as a spider's web'. After one visit the proconsul confronted his wife, reminded her of her marriage vows and said that he had done nothing to harm her. Warming to his theme, he promised that if they could only resume the intimacy they once enjoyed, he could release Andrew. Even if she did not accept him back, he could never harm her, he promised; but should she reject him, he would have no other option but to torture Andrew in the most horrible way. Think over the advantages for everyone concerned, he added, and tell me what you have decided in the morning . . .

It was a clever piece of emotional blackmail, and when Maximilla went straight round to Andrew and confessed all, the apostle was implacable. She must not yield to the 'flattery and deceitful hypocrisy', nor give herself in 'copulation with that worshipper of idols'. The apostle was defiant: 'Let him deliver me to the beasts of the north, or burn me in the fire, or drown me in the deep, or cut me with a saw or hang me upon a cross – let him know how much is our love because of Christ who has loved us in excess. We shall endure all because of fear of him and share in his true kingdom.'

Overhearing this testimony was Stratokles, Aegeates' brother, who was deeply moved. 'Your words are like arrows of fire shot in my heart,' he afterwards told Andrew. 'My thorny and dried-up soul is levelled and prepared for the seeds of your saving words.' Andrew replied that he was happy his words had met with this response but that Stratokles should know that tomorrow he would be crucified when Aegeates, the 'homicidal serpent', heard that his wife would not submit to his blackmail. Sure enough, Aegeates pronounced a death sentence, first ordering Andrew to be flogged. As he was being dragged to the place of execution, Stratokles overtook the guards and ripped their clothes off their backs before walking hand in hand with Andrew to his cross. The apostle told his new convert that he wanted him not to give evil for evil but to turn the other cheek.

The execution was due to take place by the seashore, and when he saw the cross on which he was to die, Andrew uttered a hymn in its praise because it would enable him to share the fate of his master. The guards did not break his legs when they hung him up, so that his agony would be prolonged and dogs might feed on his flesh in the night. But Andrew was far from finished. Preaching from his cross, he mesmerised the crowd, and their anger rose against Aegeates. 'Be merciful to a pious man,' they pleaded. 'He has been hanging for two days without food and yet he refreshes us with his words.' Aegeates brushed aside their pleas, but when a riot ensued that looked like ending in an uprising, Aegeates rushed off to give the order to cut down the apostle.

Andrew would have none of it. 'Let no man free me from

these bonds, for it is so fated that I now depart the body and be present with the Lord, with whom I am being crucified. This shall be accomplished!' Turning to Aegeates, Andrew told the crowd he would receive his just reward in the fires of hell. They roared at the proconsul to save Andrew, and as he stood, stunned, at the foot of the cross, Andrew delivered a dying 'aria'. 'Take me in in peace to Thy eternal tents. May my going out become a going into Thee by the many, akin to me, who rest in Thy majesty.' The date was the thirtieth of November.

Maximilla stepped forward and took down his body and had it buried by the seashore ('where the prison is'). She left Aegeates to live separately as a Christian. Andrew's death proved the final breaking-point not only for their marriage but for the proconsul's sanity. Soon afterwards, he flung himself from the roof of his praetorium.

The next chronicle of Andrew's exploits is the Acts of Andrew and Matthias. Some have argued it is based on the rescue of Matthias described above but is given a different setting and details. The book begins with the apostles drawing lots to decide which mission field should be allocated to them. Matthias (in some texts mistakenly changed to Matthew) is given the 'City of the Cannibals' as his lot. In some texts this city is not given a name; in others it is the 'Land of Dogs'; in yet others, Scythia, the northern side of the Black Sea. Herodotus wrote of Scythian 'man-eating' tribes, and Aristotle refers to cannibals around the Black Sea area. In later versions the city is named as Myrmidona and therefore identified as Myrmekion, in Crimea.

Matthias, on arrival, is blinded, drugged and thrown in prison. Jesus appears and promises Andrew will rescue him within a month. As the time draws near, Jesus appears to Andrew and tells him to hurry to the City of the Cannibals, where Matthias is about to be killed and eaten. 'How can I possibly get there in time?' Andrew asks. Jesus replies that he and his disciples will find a ship if they go down to the shore next morning. Sure enough, a boat is waiting and the three men in it (actually Jesus and two guardian angels) announce that they are going to the City of the Cannibals. Andrew's request for passage is granted, but when he announces that he and his companions have no money or food, he is permitted to travel only when he discloses that as Christians they take no money themselves. Three loaves are produced for the passengers but by this time Andrew's disciples have become seasick – even though the ship has yet to set sail!

He offers them a chance to go ashore but they decline ('Away from you we become strangers to the good things the Lord has given us'). Jesus suggests to Andrew that if they are really Christians, they will lose their fear if they are reminded of the miracles done by Jesus, whereupon Andrew recounts the stilling of the storm on the Sea of Galilee. He is now aware that the ship is under way but the sea is amazingly placid. He asks the pilot (Jesus) for his nautical secret, which he himself has failed to learn in seventeen years at sea. 'It is because you are Christians,' says the pilot, and asks Andrew to explain why the Jews do not believe in the divinity of Jesus, 'for we hear this was revealed to his disciples'.

This is followed by a somewhat artificial dialogue in which Andrew recounts the New Testament miracles of Jesus to the pilot, whom he still fails to recognise as Jesus himself. Planted in this section is a somewhat anti-Semitic section written in a different style of Greek, in which a stone sphinx in a heathen temple begins to talk and accuses the high priests of denying the divinity of Jesus ('Do not say to me that I am only a carved idol, for I tell you that our temples are better than your synagogue').

The pilot then makes Andrew fall asleep and when he wakes up, he and his disciples are lying on the ground in front of the City of the Cannibals. In their dreams they have realised that Jesus brought them here, and when Jesus appears again, this time in the form of a beautiful young boy, Andrew asks what sin he committed that he did not recognise him at sea. Jesus replies it was because they doubted being able to complete the journey in three days. Andrew then enters the city and goes to the prison, where the guards fall dead as he utters a prayer. At the sign of the cross the doors open and Matthias is rescued; and the eyes of blind prisoners are opened. The pathetic sight of naked men eating grass like dumb animals meets their eyes. Over two hundred escape, but the rulers' blood-lust has been aroused. They demand that the guards' bodies should be eaten and order ships to bring back young men for food. In the city centre there is a vat for blood and a furnace to cook the flesh.

However, as the knives are raised to kill their prey, Andrew causes the killers' hands to turn to stone. The rulers are amazed, but their insatiable hunger for human flesh makes them decree a cull of senior citizens. Two hundred and fifteen are rounded up and seven chosen by lot. One of them offers the life of his small son instead of his own, which is accepted only after his daughter has been added. As the knives are raised for a second time, Andrew's prayers are again effective. The rulers are incensed and the devil appears to incite the crowd to take revenge on Andrew. 'What is making you into sheep and cattle?

Get up and kill the stranger! He is the man who freed the prisoners. Now go and look for him so you can eat the rest of your food!'

Andrew comes out to confront the crowd (to allow the evil in them to be shown). They seize him and, deciding that roasting him is not painful enough punishment, drag him through the streets with a rope until his flesh is torn and his blood 'flowed like water on the ground'. They throw him, tied up, into prison, where the devil and seven demons arrive to taunt him – 'Where now is your power, your fearlessness, your glory?' The next day the torture begins again, as Andrew is dragged around the city at the end of a rope tied around his neck, until he cries out, 'Lord Jesus the Anointed, these tortures are enough, for I am exhausted. Thou hast seen how the enemy has mocked me with his demons and thou art mindful of thy three days upon the cross when, being little-souled, thou said, "My Father, why hast thou forsaken me?" ' (This passage referring to the torture of Andrew and Jesus and their human reactions contrasts with the Gnostic Acts of Andrew in which the non-human, divine side of Christ is emphasised.)

In despair, Andrew cries out that Jesus promised that 'they shall not touch one hair of your heads' (Luke 21:18). At last the Lord appears. Fruit-bearing trees spring up where Andrew's flesh and blood have touched the ground. Jesus touches his hand, and he stands up, restored to health. Turning to the alabaster statue of a man in the prison, Jesus spreads out his hands seven times, makes the sign of the cross and a flood pours out of it. The citizens flee. Their children and cattle drown, and they rush to the prison to free Andrew. Among them is the man who offered his son to the cannibals, now begging forgiveness. Andrew rebukes him, 'How can you say,

"Have mercy on me", when you did not have mercy on your children? You and the executioners will remain in Hell until I return and bring you back up.'

Andrew then restores the dead to life, plans a church and baptises, but as he is planning to leave, Jesus (again as the little boy) appears to persuade him to stay on and complete his mission, which ends happily as the damned men are brought up from Hell.

The Acts of Peter and Andrew is a kind of sequel to both the Acts of Andrew and the Acts of Andrew and Matthias. Upon the arrival of the two apostle brothers at the Land of the Barbarians, the devil exclaims, 'Woe to us, for here are some of the twelve Galileans who practise magic on men, for they separate women from their husbands.' The devil puts a lecherous lady in the gateway to stop them as they enter the city. Andrew prays and the Archangel Michael lifts her into the air until they pass. A rich man, Onesiphorus, forces the apostles to make a camel go through the eye of a needle, and he is converted, giving his money to the poor. The wanton woman comes down to earth as a convert and sets up a nunnery.

The Acts of Andrew and Philemon is a sequel to the Peter and Andrew story. Some versions set it in the lands of the Kurds and the city of Lydda. Peter has already converted half the city, and Andrew and Philemon are to accomplish the rest. The latter sings so sweetly in church that even some pagan priests who have come to kill the Christians are converted. While Andrew is baptising five thousand people, the devil causes a nobleman's son (in some versions he is a sheikh) to be killed by John. This man holds John's son hostage while he goes to look for Andrew. Andrew sends Philemon, who is arrested by the governor, Rufus, at the devil's instigation. His sweet voice cannot gain his release even if he brings tears to the soldiers' eyes.

But his chaste principles have not deserted him. A sparrow offers to carry a message to Andrew on Philemon's behalf. He refuses on the grounds that 'You are a fornicator, and you will not hasten your return, for if you meet a hen of your own kind, you will stay with her.' A raven is also refused (on the grounds that the raven which Noah sent on a scouting mission didn't return), but eventually a dove is deemed an acceptable carrier.

Rufus is converted, but the devil prompts his wife to kill their children. On learning this, Rufus goes to stay with Philemon, who, at the appearance of Andrew, is able to resurrect the dead children. The boy tells of a visit to Hell (Gehenna), where a house was being built for his father to burn in after his death. Jesus (in the form of a young boy) pardons the father and orders the house to be destroyed and another one built in Heaven. Rufus, now aware the house was for him, is converted on the spot. His homicidal wife is found holding in her hand a Negro who confesses to being the demon Magana. Andrew promptly banishes him to Hell, heals the woman and is set to leave. Rufus becomes his disciple, assisting at the cure of a man possessed by demons, giving his wealth to the poor and laughing at the emperor's messengers who arrive too late to confiscate his riches.

The Acts of Andrew and Bartholomew is clearly another version of the Andrew and Matthias legend. Rufus is now one of Andrew's disciples and joins the expedition to the Land of the Barbarians. In this version Jesus flies them there rather than taking the sea journey. Gallio, the governor of the city, organises a contest between the apostles and the pagan priests.

The apostles make the idols fly to the top of the temple, where they confess they are not gods. The devil incites the crowd to burn the apostles, which they fail to do. Finally they are stoned and thrown from the walls unconscious. Jesus provides a convert – a man with a dog's head – by surrounding him with fire, and he returns to the city with the apostles, killing eleven lions and two tigers which attack them. The Lord surrounds the city with fire and the people, afraid of Dog's Head and the fire, surrender and become Christians. Andrew kicks a statue, which pours forth water for the baptisms.

The Acts of Andrew and Paul continue the anti-Semitism of Acts of Andrew and Andrew and Matthias that is absent in the shorter and derivative versions. They survive only in a Coptic fragment. Accompanying Andrew on his missions, Paul dives into the sea to visit Amente (the Land of the Dead). The captain of their ship, Appolonius, cures his blind mother accidentally with Paul's cloak, while Andrew goes off at the request of a father to cure his twelve-year-old son. But the Jews refuse him entry to the city, and the boy dies. Andrew tells the father not to bury him yet and returns to the ship.

Paul is still missing in the Land of the Dead. Shown where he entered the water, Andrew prays and throws a cup of fresh water, which splits the sea, and Paul returns with a piece of wood from Amente.

His report on who was left in the punishment cells of the Underworld gives interesting insights into who were the heroes and villains for the Copts of the time. Judas Iscariot was almost alone, except for some murderers, magicians and throwers of little children into water! The rest have been rescued by Jesus. Judas was still being punished because of his suicide and for having a pact with Satan.

Still refused entry to the city, the apostles send a scarab (beetle) to the dead boy's father. (This is a pun, as the Greek words for 'scarab' and 'righteous' are very similar.) The Jews are under pressure to allow them entry but persuade the governor to suggest to the apostles that they open the gates themselves if their mission is God-given. Paul hits the gates with his Amente wood and they disappear. The dead boy has been restored to life, but the Jews have prepared a fraudulent resuscitation of their own. However, the 'dead' man confesses to the apostles. Andrew accuses the Jews of trickery and a mass conversion of 27,000 takes place. In another fragment an incident involving a woman killing her child and feeding it to her dog is included. A happy ending ensues when the pieces of the child are reassembled, laughing and weeping.

There remains one further fragment to be revealed. The story is brief: Andrew goes to Scythia and preaches in the city of Axis. Messengers are sent to persuade him to leave but are converted by the apostle. The rulers threaten to burn Andrew alive but are themselves burned by heavenly fire. Some evildoers survive and throw Andrew into prison. He prays for their destruction, but the Lord tells Andrew his work is finished. The next day the people take him out to be crucified and throw stones at him until he dies.

Is this simply an aberration, which kills off Andrew in Scythia and omits the lengthy traditional martyrdom in Achaea (at Patras)? Scythia is not named in the Egyptian texts of Andrew and Matthias, but here we have the earliest tradition of a mission to Scythia by Andrew combined with a martyrdom story. Are all the rest embellishments, and is the simple truth to be found here, that Andrew went north to the Black Sea and died there as a martyr? We will be in a better position to give an answer to that question when we have done our detective work on the texts and examined the motives of those who wrote them.

4

Andrew the Martyr

One of the agreed facts about Andrew is that he was both saint and martyr. The terms were often interchangeable in the early Christian era, but what did they originally mean? The word 'martyr' is Greek and literally means 'witness'. The first Christian martyr was Stephen, stoned to death after 'witnessing' to his faith in Acts, chapter 7. He is referred to by Paul as a 'martyr' of Christ (Acts 22:20). In Christianity the word 'martyr' took on a new and heroic meaning as more and more Christians died for their faith in the imperial persecutions, and those who died in this way came, in later years, to be honoured with a cult.

'Saint' is a precise term today, and there is a particular list of requirements which must be fulfilled before a saint can be canonised by the Pope, including well-attested miracles associated with the cult of the person. In the New Testament it was used much less precisely. The ordinary Greek word for holy is *hieros* but in Christian contexts the word *hagios* is employed. It was used in the Greek version of the Old Testament for the holiness of God but also to describe holy things and the holy people, Israel. Paul uses it (for example, in Philippians 1:1 or Ephesians 5:3) to describe the whole Christian community much in the same way that the Mormons refer to their faithful as the Church of Jesus Christ of Latter-day Saints.

The title of 'saint' began as a widely used term and only later took on the precise definition of an exceptional person. In the early Church the practice of referring to someone as *hagios* or *sanctus* (the Latin equivalent) was a mark of respect which went with their title or office. The same might be said of the use of the word 'blessed' (*beatus* in Latin), which meant originally 'rich', then 'dead', because happy and beyond troubles, but in a Christian context came to mean 'rich in blessing' because salvation had been attained in death. By any standard Andrew qualifies for the title of saint as first-called disciple, apostle, evangelist and martyr.

Those who were both saints and martyrs attracted a following – a cult – after their death. As Ursula Hall puts it:

> The triumphant death of the martyr was a vindication and a strengthening of Christian faith; an experience which bridged man's sense of separateness from God, the gap between heaven and earth. The physical relics of the martyr were the continuing evidence that this marvellous link had been made and that it could continue to be of spiritual and even practical benefit to the faithful. In the case of St Andrew, Gregory of Tours writes: 'From the tomb comes manna like flour and oil . . . the amount shows the barrenness or fertility of the coming season.' (p. 23)

Judging by the flood of pilgrims to the sites of modern manifestations such as Knock or Medjugorje, the willingness to venerate people and places that seem to provide a gateway to heaven is undiminished.

Andrew would inevitably have acquired a cult following

both as a saint and as a martyr, and relics of his body would have been the focus of this. Before we deal with the matter of what happened to his bones, we must ask the hard question – did he really die a martyr's death at Patras? The evidence is not at all supportive of the idea that he did. The oldest literature (long before the Acts of Andrew recounted in the previous chapter) that mentions Andrew is attributed to Origen and supports the idea of a mission to Scythia but has nothing to say about Achaea. His silence carries weight in that he had been in close contact with that country in AD 230 and 240. Had he been acquainted with Andrew's mission in Achaea or his death at Patras, he would surely have mentioned these in his account of the apostle's activities. The conclusion is hard to avoid – that the story of the martyrdom at Patras did not exist in Origen's era.

Further doubts arise when the names of the proconsuls in the story (Lesbius and Aegeates) are scrutinised. They are Greek names, not Latin, as one would expect for Roman officials. F. Dvornik, in his book *The Idea of Apostolicity in Byzantium and the Legend of the Apostle Andrew*, argues this point strongly, adding that even if it is allowed that Achaea was governed between AD 44 and 67 by proconsuls, under a mandate of the Roman Senate, it is most unlikely that they resided in Patras. Corinth was more likely to be the residence of a Roman governor, as the first colony in Achaea and the most important trading centre.

The stories about Andrew preaching in the region also conflict with other more reliable reports on the development of the Christian community there. St Paul was the key figure in planting churches there. He founded the community at Corinth and his exploits feature in the earliest available accounts of the growth of the Christian Church written by Paul's aide, St Luke the Evangelist. According to an old prologue to St Luke's Gospel (which features in some texts), it was written 'in the regions of Achaea'. Although it is possible that Andrew visited Achaea and died at Patras, it would be extremely strange if Luke had omitted this significant fact. The conclusion drawn by Dvornik is that Andrew did not visit there at all.

A further piece of circumstantial evidence is provided by Dvornik in the shape of a document written outside Greece in the fourth century. It is the Syriac 'Teaching of the Apostles', whose sources, it claims, are the apostles: 'What James had written from Jerusalem, and Simon from the city of Rome, and John from Ephesus, and Mark from great Alexandria, and Andrew from Phrygia, and Luke from Macedonia, and Judas Thomas from India'. The author goes on to review the missionary activity of the apostles:

> Ephesus and Thessalonica and all Asia and all the country of the Corinthians and all Achaea and its environs received the apostle's hand of priesthood from JOHN the Evangelist, who had leaned on the bosom of our Lord and who built a church there and ministered there in his office of guide.
>
> Nicaea and Nicomedia and all the country of Bithynia and of Gothia, and of the regions around it, received the apostle's hand of priesthood from ANDREW, the brother of Simon Cephas who was guide and ruler in the church he built there and was priest and ministered there.
>
> Byzantium and all the country of Thrace and its environs even to the great river, the border which separates the barbarians, received the apostle's hand from

LUKE the Apostle who built a church there and was priest and ministered there in his office of ruler and guide.

A quick look at the map on p. 26 shows that this puts Luke where he always was, John where other reliable traditions put him and Andrew back into the Black Sea area. How then did he end up as a martyr in Patras?

One possible explanation is that the Achaioi, a tribe in the Caucasus along the Black Sea coast from Scythia, were confused with the Achaeans. The Caucasian tribe were well known in the classical period, sometimes identified as refugees from Troy (by the Greek historian Strabo).

On the other hand, perhaps the confusion was deliberate. Dvornik suggests that the author of the Acts of Andrew, familiar with the tradition putting Andrew in Scythia, used the name of this tribe to link Andrew with Patras to provide him with a climax to the apostle's life story, especially one that paralleled the heroic martyrdom of his brother Peter. Ending their days in obscurity was not the stuff of which apostles were made. A glorious martyrdom was far more appropriate and, Dvornik suggests, such a cult may have already been started around a local saint in Patras. Borrowing the details of one saint and ascribing them to another seems unscrupulous, but it was not uncommon (as we shall see when we come to the legend of St Regulus and his part in the life of St Andrew). Dvornik's conclusion is that the Acts of Andrew, whose climax is the Achaean visit and Patras martyrdom, is an elaborate myth constructed for several purposes – one of which was to provide its hero with a suitable martyrdom. The work could not have been composed in the second century but only after Origen, at the end of the third. The legend then went through various stages in which it was edited and added to by various hands in East and West, using it to promote their idea of Andrew and in turn Andrew to promote their ideas.

It is a saga of art creating history and of history imitating art. Disentangling the fact and the fiction has given rise to a scholarly jigsaw puzzle. I have never been very good at jigsaws, but conventional wisdom says you start at the corners. In the case of texts in the early Church there were four corners of language: Syriac, Greek, Latin, Coptic. These represented different geographic and cultural aspects of the developing faith, Middle Eastern, Hellenistic, Roman, Egyptian, centred on the important cities for early Christianity – Antioch, Ephesus, Rome, Alexandria. Then there was Jerusalem – the starting point for a faith that began as Jewish but rapidly became 'Gentilised' and dispersed throughout the world around the Mediterranean. Next tip for jigsaw solving is to assemble the pieces with the same colour. Looking at the ideas that coloured thinking in this epoch, there are at least three that are reflected in the Acts of Andrew. First is the anti-Semitism that identifies Jews who did not become Christians as the people who killed Jesus; second is the Gnosticism that is reflected in miracle stories portraying Christ (and his apostles) as scarcely human or bound by natural laws; third is the ascetic thinking that arose in the monastic movement of the third century and is seen in the Acts of Andrew stories in which celibacy and chastity are seen as superior to monogamy.

There are some pieces which do not fit so easily into the jigsaw. The installation of Stachys as Bishop of Byzantium (see the summary from the Narratio on p. 27) does not appear in the omnibus edition of the miracles of Andrew made by

Gregory of Tours (*c.* AD 591–2). Eusebius, the father of church history (AD 265–339), was not aware of it either, apparently. For centuries after the Acts of Andrew first appeared churchmen in East and West seem to have behaved as if this important incident had not occurred. The conclusion is that the episode involving the consecration of Stachys is a forgery.

Continuing in our role as literary detectives, we need first to seek a motive for inserting such a forgery into the Acts of Andrew. We find our motive by looking at the history of rivalry between Roman and Byzantium (the New Rome), renamed Constantinople in honour of its founder, Emperor Constantine, who made the key decision to adopt Christianity as the official religion of the empire in AD 312. The once-persecuted Jewish sect was now the established faith. By the fifth century the minority status of the past was long forgotten and popes Leo the Great and Gelasius had hammered home the supremacy of Rome, first among sees, arbiter of orthodoxy, the legatee of Peter, etc. New Rome, despite having been the creation of the emperor, lacked ecclesiastical clout to go with this role. It was necessary to create an anti-Peter, a counterweight to the supremacy of Rome. Such a candidate would possess an authority handed down directly from the original group of disciples – what is known as apostolic succession. Andrew was ripe for the role, but not before a few centuries had yellowed his bones. At first there seems to have been apathy about Andrew in the Eastern Church, then a period in which he was promoted more in the West before the forger got to work.

Constantinople could not boast the tomb of St Peter, keeper of the keys, but it had the Church of the Holy Apostles, burial place of the emperors, which housed the bones of Luke and Paul's disciple Timothy. According to Jerome, they were put there, along with Andrew's bones, in 356–7 by Constantine's son, Constantius. In 370 Constantine's remains were transferred to the Church of the Holy Apostles and the emperors became 'doorkeepers to the fishermen'. However, the early years of this process were not ones in which Andrew became a focus of pretension. St John Chrysostom, Bishop of Constantinople 398–404, does not make direct reference to the relics and states that the only apostles whose burial places were known during his lifetime were Peter, Paul, John and Timothy. This suggests that the bones of Andrew may have arrived at a later date. His predecessor, Gregory of Nazianos (bishop 378–81) refers only briefly to Andrew and his mission in Greece.

Even during the Acacian schism between Rome and Constantinople (485–519) there was no sign of Andrew being a source of rivalry. Indeed, the cult of Andrew was growing apace in the Western (Latin) Church. In Rome an oratory on the Via Labicana and a basilica on the Esquiline, both dedicated to Andrew, appeared during this period. Relics of Andrew begin to appear in Italy. In 394 Bishop Ambrose of Milan dedicated relics of St Andrew, St John and St Thomas in the Church of the Holy Apostles in Milan, which already contained relics of St Peter and St Paul. They were a gift from his ally Pope Damasus and survive to this day in a silver casket known as the St Nazaro reliquary. When opened in 1579 it apparently contained cloth, not bones. These may be *brandea*, curiously described as 'second-class' relics – pieces of cloth which were wrapped around the originals and were supposed to acquire some of their spiritual qualities.

It is probable that Ambrose was instrumental in placing other relics in Italy as a kind of holy antique dealer. Among these were Andrean relics, and by the early fifth century Brescia,

Aquileia, Nola and Fundi claimed to have relics of the apostle. Paulinus, a government official and poet from Gaul, who became a Christian and was bishop at Nola in southern Italy from 409, gives an insight into the way in which relics were regarded at this time. He writes of Constantine's plan to defend the walls of his new city with the body of Andrew (Poem 19) and in Poem 27: 'Whenever there is part of a saint's body, there too his power emerges.' He refers to sacred ashes being scattered like seeds of life in many places. The implication is that relics could be quite small, even particles, and that we should not be thinking of actual parts of the body being involved.

Andrew's beard turned up a century later in Ravenna as a result of the pretensions of Theodoric the Great, king of the Ostrogoths, who had in common with Andrew the fact that they both sought Christian converts in Scythia. One suspects that the warrior king's style of persuasion differed slightly from Andrew's and owed more to the Attila the Hun school of evangelism. Theodoric built the church of St Andrew of the Goths in Ravenna, and the beard was acquired by Bishop Maximian from Constantinople.

As we shall see in chapter 6, the cult of Andrew in the West was given another boost by Gregory the Great (Pope 590–604). Up to this point there seems to have been no attempt to challenge the supremacy of Rome and to use Andrew as the first-called apostle in order to do it. The idea of claiming Andrew back for the East was a bold and clever move.

Dorotheus was a bishop of Tyre living at the time of Constantine, but around 800 a text appeared under his name which purported to be a list of bishops of Byzantium. It began from the time at which Andrew apparently ordained Stachys and continued up to the first hitherto recorded bishop (Metrophanes, who features in the Chronicon Paschale as the first bishop in 313). Since it defies credibility that such a list would have been ignored by all and sundry for 500 years if it genuinely existed at the time of Constantinople's foundation as the New Rome, the document is known as Pseudo-Dorotheus.

His partner in crime, Pseudo-Epiphanius (named after the original monk of Callistratos, in Constantinople, who died in 402), apparently compiled a life of St Andrew, which became known in a more polished form as the Laudatio. It contains the Stachys legend. His praise for Andrew is balanced by respect for Peter, and the impression is given that the world was divided between them. This has led some scholars to put on the document the date of 880, which marked the end of the Photian schism between the rival Rome and Constantinople Churches, the reason being that Patriarch Photios was anxious to make a deal and re-establish relations between the two centres.

Two facts emerge strongly from all of this. Andrew was conspicuous by his absence for several centuries from the Greek area of influence, which was later to claim him as its own over against Rome. He was, if anything, more actively revered in the West until the eighth and ninth centuries. The works whose authenticity is in question appeared around then in the Eastern Church and became the accepted version of Andrew's life. In the West the Gregory (of Tours) version continued to be enjoyed, but no mention of the 'pseudo-apostolic' line surfaces until 1586 (when Stachys is credited in a Vatican martyrology), long after the rivals finally and irrevocably split from one another in 1054.

Meanwhile the Orthodox Church was ensuring the durability of the Andrew legends. Among these were the Synaxaria (eleventh century); the Menologion of Basil (tenth century); and an anonymous work that identified the church of St Irene at Galata as the building in which Andrew ordained Stachys. From the tenth century on, Byzantium accepted the Pseudo-Dorotheus and -Epiphanius legends as the only true tradition. At this point the Georgians became acquainted with the legends and adopted them. In 988, when Russia embraced the Orthodox faith, it swallowed the legends whole and even managed to add a few of its own, as we shall see in the next chapter.

5

Svetoi Andrei –

Patron Saint of Russia

The adjective 'Byzantine' is occasionally applied to arguments as well as styles of architecture. The expression 'It matters not one iota' derives from one such dispute about the Nicene Creed, drawn up to unite all centres against the followers of Arius, who taught that only God the Father could be described as divine.

Some were inclined to fudge the question of what substance Christ actually consisted but with the Emperor Constantine looking on and banging heads together, the Council of Nicaea in 325 tried (unsuccessfully, as it turned out) to put an end to years of theological battles in which Christ was defined as having two natures in one body, or one nature (divine) in a human body, or an apparently human body, or an apparently divine body. These attempts had not clarified the issue. To define Christ's precise relationship with God the phrase 'like substance' (Greek: *homoi-ousios*) was proposed, but the opponents of Arius were having none of it. Nicaea insisted that Christ was one substance with God and only the phrase *homo-ousios* ('same-substance') would do. The difference was one letter 'i', the Greek letter *iota* – and it certainly mattered at the time.

In general, the way in which the East approached these questions was different from the West's. A comparison could be made with the contrasting approaches to diplomacy of

European nations and the USA. We might expect Andrew to have been taken up – as the forgers possibly intended – to be an anti-Peter and used as the basis of authority in the way Rome used Peter. But, paradoxically, this did not happen in Greece. Local leadership and the cult of local saints seem to have played a more significant role in the Eastern Church. Perhaps this explains why Andrew enjoys an honoured place in the Greek Orthodox liturgy and is the patron saint of Greece – but does not have the same status as Peter does for Catholics.

This difference in style was shown right from the beginning of the adoption of Christianity as the official religion of the Roman empire in 312. The bones of Andrew were considered important enough to be brought to the New Rome, but the great churches there were still dedicated to abstractions – for example, Eirene (peace), Sophia (wisdom), Dynamis (power) – plus one to Archangel Michael and four to local saints and martyrs. Andrew continued to be revered as the local saint of Patras, but throughout Greece his profile remained modest – something which may have pleased the retiring Andrew we met in the Gospels.

However, in the tenth century, just when the Pseudo-Dorotheus and Pseudo-Epiphanius legends were gaining currency, a significant development took place to the north. Prince Vladimir of Kiev was a coming man seeking to consolidate a kingdom and integrate the peoples under his sway. This ambition was not harmed by his forthcoming marriage to Anna, sister of Emperor Basil at Constantinople. There are various stories about how he came to adopt Christianity as the official religion of his country, which he accomplished in autocratic fashion by ordering a mass baptism of the populace in the River Dnieper at Kiev.

Those who believe that behind every successful man stands a woman will no doubt favour the explanation that Anna influenced him with bedchamber evangelism and perhaps some bedchamber diplomacy. I prefer the story that Vlad sent emissaries off to various countries to find the most appropriate form of religion for his up-and-coming nation. They reached Constantinople and were so overwhelmed by the beauty of sight, sound and smell that they encountered in the church of Santa Sophia that they felt themselves to be at the very gate of Heaven. Vlad was glad to take their advice and thus founded the Church whose roots were in Byzantium but whose branches eventually stretched into every corner of the vast empire that became Russia.

It was Constantinople rather than Rome he was acknowledging and its system of Caesaro-papism in which the Church is part of the fabric of state. As the state Church of a great nation, the new Russian Orthodox Church was only too pleased to learn that Andrew, one of the original inner group of apostles, had visited the Kievan Rus. It embraced the legends of the Acts of Andrew, the ones added by Pseudo-Dorotheus and Pseudo-Epiphanius, and was able to supply a few of its own. Enter Svetoi Andrei, the patron saint of Russia.

The Russian Primary Chronicle dates from the eleventh or twelfth century. It describes how Andrew went from Byzantium by the shore of the Black Sea to Scythia (south of Russia) and then Crimea. Under divine guidance he sailed up the River Dnieper, which emerges there, and stopped overnight among the hills around Kiev. In the morning he told his disciples: 'Believe me, on these hills the goodness of God will shine; a great city will be here and God will create many churches and enlighten the whole of Russia with holy baptisms.'

Having prayed all night, in the morning Andrew climbed the hills, blessed them and erected a cross, prophesying the adoption by the people there of the faith of his apostolic Church established in Byzantium. The Chronicle notes – with the benefit of hindsight – that this had indeed happened (with Prince Vladimir's action in 988). (Later biographies of the saints of Russia state confidently that the exact spot on which Andrew erected his cross is now the site of the Church of Apostle Andrew, First-called, in Kiev.)

Astonishingly, the Chronicle goes on to describe how Andrew then went to Novgorod to evangelise there. Since Novgorod is half-way between Moscow and St Petersburg and a thousand kilometres from Kiev, this stretches credulity as well as endurance. The legend came to be used by Novgorod in the fourteenth century to assert its independence from Constantinople's jurisdiction, on the grounds that the Church there had been personally founded by Andrew.

There he encounters the sauna bath, which he regards as a horrific form of masochism to be resisted by all good Christians. Saunas have acquired a dubious reputation in red-light areas in modern cities, but Andrew's objections were more basic: 'They have wooden bath-houses which the people heat until they are red-hot. They then undress, and, after pouring over themselves *kvas* (a beery drink made from mouldy bread), they take young twigs and lash their bodies so much that they can hardly move. Half-dead, they pour icy water over themselves and only then are revived. They do this daily. Tortured by nobody, they instead torture themselves and call it washing!'

This somewhat jaundiced account of the sauna culture Andrew found among the Slavs of Novgorod perhaps owes more to the fact that the author of the Chronicle had a motive in pouring some cold water of his own on their pretensions! In this account in the Russian Primary Chronicle, Andrew is said also to have visited the land of the Varangians (Norsemen), then made his way to Rome, where he recounted his adventures, before going east to his fate at Patras. How credible is this legend? Wholly credible, according to Petrov Sergei, Metropolitan of Odessa and Kherson, in a lecture given in 1988, when he was awarded a doctorate by the Orthodox Theology Faculty of Preshov in the Czech Republic. I leave readers to judge whether they find his account, given here in translation, a plausible one:

In Odessa we have a divinity faculty, the Odessa Spiritual Seminary, which counts St Apostle Andrew as its higher guardian, reflecting the ancient belief of our Church that St Andrew came this way when the south of Ukraine and Dnieper were inhabited by Skifs (the people of Scythia). The similarity of this record and the church-wide legends about the preaching in Scythia of the first-called disciple of Christ would seem to provide adequate historical and scientific grounds for believing that the apostle preached in our land too. But since the middle of the eighteenth century there has appeared some literature that is sceptical of this legend. The famous Church historian E. E. Golubinski sums up three (as he thought, very strong) arguments.

First, beyond Scythia was barren wilderness, unknown to the rest of the world, and so it was impossible for the apostle to have travelled there.

Second, the sauna episode is out of tune with the serious tone of the Chronicle. Different regions of Russia teased each other with sarcastic stories, and this sounds like one.

Third, in the Chronicle there is an older narrative that says, 'In the land of Russia, the apostles did not teach,' and 'The apostles were not here in bodily presence.' Thus the legend about Andrew was inserted later.

Scientists and sceptics therefore consider the creation of the legend of Andrew's visiting Russia as the act of vanity of one author who wanted to portray Russians as among the first to receive Christianity. However, not all of their arguments are sustainable. Regarding the first point above, it has been shown that it was wrong to consider the lands beyond the Dnieper as wild and unknown to the rest of the world. They were part of trade routes used by the Greeks in the first century BC. As for points two and three, the Christian faith has no doubt about the validity of the legend that Andrew preached in Russia because it was supported by the Church, the guardian of truth. Thus we consider this legend true, and all scientific attempts to prove otherwise are only hypotheses because science does not have the means to prove or disprove the truth of this legend . . .

If Scythia was known to the Greeks and Romans as part of the universe, then surely the apostles, who were very thorough in following the prophecy contained in the Old Testament that the future Messiah's teaching would spread to the end of the universe, would have tried to reach it. There is also the prophecy of Christ himself ('Go ye into all nations'). Given the very nature of Andrew, his spiritual commitment, one imagines that he would have been very eager to fulfil the wishes of Christ;

it is understandable that it was he who came to Russia. Can you imagine him reaching the southern borders of our land, then suddenly deciding to turn back?

Further, we consider that if someone had forged the Chronicle, then they would have copied the style of the important legends and certainly would not have added a ridiculous story about a sauna. It proves the originality of the story. The storyteller simply had to record what had happened and what was said.

Another argument for the authenticity of the sauna episode is that pagans had a cult of the body and valued highly everything to do with it (including bathing). This is apparent from the famous Roman baths – they were palaces.

The main aim of the apostles' preaching was to make people admit their own sins and be baptised in the name of Christ. Andrew may have drawn on the contrasting images of washing the body in a bath and washing the soul by confessing sins. That is another reason for believing that he did refer to bathing habits.

So the Apostle did preach on Russian land, up to Novgorod, but his preaching did not bear much fruit. Christianity was not accepted at that time. That is why it is understandable that Andrew felt like an alien among strangers and a little bitter when talking about the bathing habits of the barbarians, remembering the words of Holy Scripture, 'Light came into the world but people liked darkness rather than light because their acts were evil.' The pagans of the north preferred the dubious pleasures of the bath to life eternal and Christ's cross. This was the thinking Andrew expressed in his report on this journey. It is mentioned several times in Holy Scripture that such a report existed. [The Metropolitan then cites Acts 11:4–18, 15:12, 21:19; Galatians 2:1–2.]

The story of the bath episode was incorporated into the Chronicle by the outstanding theologian and historian Nestor at the end of the eleventh or the beginning of the twelfth century. Although Christianity had been introduced into Russia a century previously, pagan superstitions were still alive. Nestor used the sauna-bath episode from an original report about a journey in Russia by Andrew as religious satire to condemn this superstition.

It is noteworthy that the people of Novgorod had to be baptised by fire and the sword, while the people of Kiev were baptised quickly and without problems. Later (in 1074–8) almost all the citizens of Novgorod were nominal Christians but switched to the side of a pagan during a revolt.

This concludes Metropolitan Sergei's 'defence'. Quite what the citizens of Novgorod would make of it, I shudder to think – or even the former Metropolitan of Novgorod and Leningrad, Alexei, who is now Patriarch of all Russia. Reprinted in the *Journal of the Moscow Patriarchate*, vol. 7 (1988), it illustrates the different forensic standards which Orthodox leaders bring to assessing the legends of Andrew.

I came across an alternative Russian version to the out-landish claims of the Chronicle in the *Life and Labours of Saint Apostle Andrew, First-called*, published in Odessa in 1894, based on the chronicle of Russian Orthodox saints published in 1858. This follows the life of Andrew as told in the Gospels, picks up the intinerary of the Acts of Andrew, then outlines the 'third journey of Andrew'. This begins in Georgia (then called Svanetia and Osetia), where he met with success. Not so in the land of the Djigits (lawless tribes who rode everywhere on horseback). Their modern descendants are people such as the Chechens who have proved such a thorn in the flesh of modern Russia. These people met Andrew with hostility and tried to kill him. The account adds: 'They still don't have faith – punishment for treating Andrew like that.'

After this Caucasian adventure, Andrew journeyed to the Crimea, where he visited a number of towns, leaving converts behind wherever he went, and finally reached the town of Khersones. This is apparently not the modern Cherson at the mouth of the Dnieper, since the account adds that Khersones doesn't exist any more, but ruins can be seen near Sevastapol. There is a cathedral commemorating the spot where Prince Vladimir was baptised prior to the mass baptism which his people underwent at Kiev. There is also a legend that the spot where Andrew came ashore can still be identified.

The next chapter begins with Andrew expressing his desire to visit the 'land of the Goths and Skifs' and the voyage up the Dnieper to Kiev, already described. However, after erecting his cross there, it continues: 'Andrew went back, visiting places he had already visited to see if faith was still alive there. So he visited Sinope for a third time.' (This contrasts with the earlier account in the Acts of Andrew of Sinope being hostile territory and also omits any mention of places north such as Novgorod.)

Andrew continues into Greece, and the Patras martyrdom completes this saga. The two Russian hagiographies of Andrew differ in the detail of what happened after his death on the cross. In the 1894 life, Aegeates' wife, Maximilla, buried him by the seashore 'and did not leave his grave while alive'. Her unhappy husband then committed suicide by jumping from a window. The earlier account has Maximilla put Andrew into her own coffin. 'Aegeates wanted to punish her but died.' However, both are agreed that the remains were transferred to Constantinople at a much later date.

The life then states that in 1208 Pope Innocent 'gave permission to transfer the remains to Amalfi, but the head of Andrew, which was kept in Patras, was brought to Rome where it is still kept in the Cathedral of St Peter'. (This is incorrect, as we shall see in the next chapter, and so perhaps we should treat with caution the next part of the story.) 'During the time of Tsar Michael Fyodorovitch [the first of the Romanovs, whose dynasty began in 1613] Patriarch Parfeni sent him the right hand of St Andrew. The fingers are brought together for holy blessing. It was as though St Andrew wanted to show posterity how the fingers should be held for blessing and to warn people not to be misled by poor teaching.'

The account further adds that the left foot of Andrew is kept in the Ilyinsky monastery on Mount Aphos in northern Greece. First given by the emperor, in 964, to the Greek Varetad monastery, which was burnt by Turks, it was bought by the head of the Ilyinsky monastery as a contribution to restoration funds. However, we should not allow the extravagance of the Russian Primary Chronicle to blind us to the fact that time and again different strands of evidence link Andrew with the Black Sea and Crimea. Does it matter that the time gap cannot be filled in with details? As we have seen, the Andrew legend was revived by the conversion of Russia. We shall now see how new life was breathed into the bones of St Andrew in the West.

6

Dry Bones and the Westerly Wind

Whose bones were removed from Patras to Constantinople can never now be proved. If all the bits of bones alleged to be those of Andrew that are residing in various sacred sites around Europe were reassembled and then subjected to genetic finger-printing and carbon dating, I suspect there would be a miracu-lous fulfilment of Ezekiel's vision of the valley of dry bones which came to life. As from the rib of Adam came another person, so from the bones of Andrew would arise a whole group of new disciples/apostles. In other words, the bones would be shown to derive from a number of different people.

It would be nice to think that those who handled the bones were more scrupulous than those who rewrote the papyri and that it would be possible to put Andrew – like a holy Humpty Dumpty – together again. Alas, it is highly unlikely. Some of the relics fell into hostile hands (Turkish in the case of some Eastern relics, iconoclastic and Protestant in the case of the relics in St Andrews, Scotland); others have been broken up into pieces to be given to other centres as gifts or for money.

One thing that can be asserted, however, is that some bones were taken from Patras to Constantinople. Whether these included the head is not so certain. It was not uncommon to separate a head, being a particularly potent relic, and many boasted of having the head of an apostle, while others begged to be given one. Some kind of shrine remained at Patras (cf. Gregory of Tours' reference to this flowing with manna and a story he tells of a traveller in Patras who asked for a doctor and was directed to a 'heavenly doctor who could cure without medicine' and, upon praying at Andrew's tomb, was promptly cured). Ursula Hall found references to an olive tree at Patras which was revered as the tree on which Andrew was crucified (*St Andrew and Scotland*, p. 81) and points out that there was a church of St Andrew at Patras from the Byzantine period, restored by Bishop Malatesta in 1426, for which Dufay wrote the motet *Apostolo glorioso*. This church was on the site of the temple of Demeter and nearby was a sacred spring, identified as St Andrew's Well to the Scots historian W. Skene when he visited Patras in 1844.

When another Scottish scholar, Principal Tulloch of St Andrews, visited Patras at the turn of the century he asked his diary 'Did Andrew ever live and labour here? Are his bones still lying there, as the stranger is assured, in the plain wooden coffer in the white cathedral church near the shore by the holy well that bears his name? All the devout of Patras profoundly believe this and flock thither on the anniversary of the saint, lighting the sacred shrine with their tapers as they invoke his guardian care. Or were his apostolic remains transported to Amalfi, as the good Catholics of southern Italy believe, while they point with confidence to the noble church which rises above their supposed resting place? Or did St Rule carry them off to St Andrews and build a shrine for them there and rear a national Christianity on this devout hypothesis? Hopeless as these questions are for the historian, they are beautiful to the imagination. . . I felt that morning at Patras as if St Andrew were a more living character than I had before realised him to be' (quoted in *St Andrew: the Disciple, the Missionary, the Patron Saint*, Peter Ross, p. 60).

Perhaps that reflection by a presbyterian whose Church has not been known for giving excessive honour to the saints carries the best of all sentiments – a proper balance between forensic fact and piety in dealing with St Andrew. When Principal Tulloch visited Patras the head of Andrew that now graces the new Cathedral of St Andrew at Patras was certainly not there. A church was completed in 1979 partly to give honoured place to a head which was presented to Patras in 1964 by Pope Paul VI as an ecumenical gesture.

This head had followed a circuitous route. When Andrew's bones were taken to Constantinople by Artemius on Constantius' orders, the head was either left at Patras or returned there by a generous emperor at a subsequent date. It was certainly there by the medieval period, during which the Turks invaded Achaea in 1453. To safeguard the precious relic, Thomas Palaeologus, a member of the Achaean nobility, fled to Corfu with the head, and it was acquired by Pope Pius II, anxious to use it as a catalyst for a new crusade against the Turks. Brought to St Peter's in Rome with great ceremony on 11 April 1462, it was housed in a reliquary. The event is immortalised on the tomb of Pius II in the church of S. Andrea della Valle, which also houses a famous Andrean painting by Domenichino in which John the Baptist points out Jesus to Andrew, Jesus calls Andrew, the executioners torture Andrew, and he is then seen worshipping the cross and, finally, being carried to heaven by angels. Here art parallels literature – in both, the Gospels are used at first, then are supplanted by the legends.

But what of the bones within the Church of the Holy Apostles in Constantinople, now known as the Fatih Camii mosque? As we have seen, there was not a lot of excitement about them in earlier centuries, and when Emperor Justinian decided to rebuild the somewhat shaky building around AD 550, there were no signs in the church of any tombs or remains. Procopius, writing in about 560, records: 'But when the workmen dug over the whole place, so that nothing unseemly should be left, three wooden coffins were discovered lying there, neglected but bearing inscriptions saying that these were the bodies of the apostles Andrew, Luke and Timothy.' With enthusiasm the bodies were reburied in a suitable place of honour. Perhaps they had already been picked over and looted. Where else could the bones and relics have come from which appeared around Italy at the end of the fourth century?

Apart from the 'second-class relics' in the reliquary, the Andrean relics at Milan seem to have disappeared. Ambrose's Church of the Holy Apostles was rebuilt in the twelfth century, as S. Nazaro Maggiore, in honour of a local martyr. However, Milan's place alongside Amalfi and St Andrews as a centre of the Andrean cult is recorded in a mosaic in Westminster Cathedral, London. The other three places depicted in the mosaic are Bethsaida, Constantinople and Patras.

Whatever the authenticity of the three coffins reburied in 550, they provided a focus for honouring St Andrew and they remained in their new resting place until 1204, when Constantinople was captured from the Turks in the Fourth Crusade and the Greek emperor replaced with a Latin one. Cardinal Peter of Capua, in his role as papal legate, used the opportunity to get hold of various relics, including the 'body of St Andrew', which was brought to Amalfi, then one of the chief Italian ports. The reconstruction of the cathedral, in which the cardinal was involved, was a suitable excuse to unveil the bones on 8

May 1208. Chronicles of the time recorded 'all knew and believed' that they were the genuine article.

The cardinal appeared to have a taste for the secretive, for he kept some of the bones aside when he buried the rest in a reliquary under the altar. These turned up in 1603 and contained the back part of a skull and some other pieces of bone. The urn was reburied, dug up again in 1846 and finally put in the crypt, where it is now available for public veneration.

Beneath the altar at Amalfi is a room surrounded by metal grilles, floored with a large stone covering the tomb of St Andrew in which is a circular hole over which a metal vessel is suspended. Since at least 1308 a thick, dewy liquid called manna has collected on the vessel. This is collected on dates associated with Andrew and is used to cure the sick. The bones still appear to have life-giving powers.

Two men have done more than anyone else to promote St Andrew in the Western Church, and both were called Gregory. Gregory of Tours we have met already. He lived from 538 to 594 and is otherwise famed for his ten-volume history of the Franks. His interest in St Andrew was personal, since his birthday was 30 November. In his prologue to his book of St Andrew's miracles he reflects that most hagiography concentrates on the death of the saint but that he has found a lengthy account of miraculous deeds by St Andrew which he proposes to edit in a way which will 'please the reader'. It no doubt also pleased the more orthodox, since Gregory's version – based largely on a Latin version of the original Greek Acts of Andrew – was purged of the heretical, Gnostic tone of the original.

His story begins with Andrew leaving Achaea for Mermidona to save Matthias from infidels (not cannibals in his version), then travelling along the southern shores of the Black Sea and visiting Sinope and Nicomedia before going on the Byzantium and, finally, Macedonia. After preaching in Philippi and Thessalonica, he is arrested by the proconsul Virinus and thrown to the lions but survives unscathed. Finally he returns to Achaea, visiting Corinth and other places, ending in Patras. There he wins over the proconsul Lesbius to Christianity, but when Lesbius is replaced by Aegeates, whose wife and brother (Maximilla and Stratokles) are converted, Andrew falls foul of Aegeates and is imprisoned, tortured and finally crucified. Throughout Gregory's story Andrew is healing the sick, casting out demons, restoring the dead to life, taking a stern line on sexuality and advocating a life of chastity. Gregory omits details of the martyrdom itself, since, he points out, it is available elsewhere.

St Andrew was not yet prominent in Western Europe beyond Italy (Gregory's history of the Franks gives a prayer calendar of Tours cathedral for the decade beginning 480, and there is no mention of Andrew), but Gregory can claim much of the credit for the saint's popularisation.

The other man who acted as an apostle of the apostle was Gregory the Great, who ended his days in 604 as Pope but began life as a young man of wealth and influence in Rome. Renouncing the world on the death of his father in 574, he turned the family mansion on the Caelian Hill into a monastery dedicated to St Andrew. (It is now the church of St Gregory the Great with an adjoining St Andrew chapel and famous paintings by Guido Reni and Domenichino. Reni's work shows Andrew worshipping the cross with the walls of Patras in the background.)

The choice of Andrew was not that extraordinary. As we have already seen, there was interest in Andrew in the fourth century in Rome. A feast of St Andrew was celebrated; there were several churches in his name; and by the end of the fifth century Pope Simplicius had adopted Andrew as his patron. One biographer of Gregory has him living simply as a monk, 'ruling jointly with St Andrew' on the Caelian Hill, but he was in for a rude shock. He was dispatched in 579 to Constantinople to work for Rome for seven years. There he would have encountered Justinian's newly rebuilt Church of the Holy Apostles with its three apostles reburied in positions of honour. There is a tradition that Gregory brought back to Rome in 586 an arm of Andrew, which was eventually housed on the Caelian Hill, but, as Ursula Hall points out (*St Andrew and Scotland*, p. 37), this is extremely unlikely given Gregory's published views on the breaking up of bodies to spread relics. Furthermore, he refused a request from Constantina, wife of the Byzantine emperor, Maurice, for a piece of the body of Paul (*Letters*, 4.40) on the grounds that bodies of the saints should not be disturbed.

In 590 Gregory became Pope and is credited with laying the foundations of what was to become the medieval papacy through his leadership and organisational skills. He was a genuinely great and selfless pope who wished to extend the Gospel to ordinary people who had not yet heard it properly. (There is a famous story that he saw flaxen-haired English boys who had become slaves in Rome and expressed the wish that these Angles could become angels. In 596 he sent Augustine, the prior of the St Andrew monastery in Rome, to Kent, where he was guaranteed a welcome by King Ethelbert. It was the start of a new chapter in the religious history of England; Andrew was to play a significant role in helping the English Church back on its feet before being claimed by Scotland.

7

From Greece to Scotland via

Rome and England

Pope Gregory's evangelisation of England brought other benefits to the papacy. In 600 the style of Christianity in the British Isles was decidedly out of tune with Roman ways. The powerhouse of the Church was Irish, and the culture was Celtic. North of the Midlands of England lay lands where it was not possible to assert the authority of the papacy. The Celtic priesthood was hereditary. Celtic monks did not employ the Roman tonsure, in which the hair was shaved from the crown of the head, but shaved in front of a line drawn from ear to ear, their prominent foreheads giving them a highbrow look. Even the date of Easter was different.

Augustine's mission on behalf of Gregory proved to be decisive for Christianity in the British Isles. Beginning in Kent, he moved north and was particularly successful in the east of England. In 664 a synod was convened at Whitby in Yorkshire to decide whose authority was to be obeyed – that of the Celtic Church or that of Rome. The argument of Petrine supremacy was used to great effect by St Wilfrid of York. St Peter, not St Columba, had been handed the keys of the kingdom of heaven by Christ, he pointed out. The result was the irresistible expansion of Roman-style Christianity. Those who found the new deal difficult to accept went west to Ireland or north-west to Iona.

Wilfrid left another legacy that was to prove decisive. Earlier in his life, when he conceived his vision of turning the north-east of England from the Columban/Celtic form of Christianity to the Roman, he had gone into a church in Rome that was dedicated to St Andrew in order to pray for success. Feeling grateful to Andrew for his subsequent success and eloquence at the decisive synod at Whitby, he dedicated to the saint his monastery at Hexham, near the spot where the north and south Tyne become one river. Wilfrid, whose chroniclers paint him as a saintly man, was a seminal figure as the influence of the Northumbrians and Angles moved northwards into Scotland.

At this time Scotland was divided into two nations: the kingdom of Dalriada lay in the west, and north of the Forth valley was the kingdom of the Picts – so called by the Romans (who failed to conquer them) because of their taste for colourful tattoos, with which they terrified their enemies as they rushed naked into battle.

To the south lay the Northumbrian kingdom from whose nobility Wilfrid of York came. Wilfrid – educated at Lindisfarne and Canterbury, like many churchmen of integrity before and since – fell foul of the ruler of his day, who disliked having a church leader whose first allegiance lay elsewhere. Despite being backed by the Pope in his difficulties with the king, Wilfrid was restored only on the king's death. Wilfrid himself died in 709.

His successor as Bishop of York was Acca, Wilfrid's protégé, who had travelled with him on visits to Rome and also revered Andrew. Acca expanded the importance of the Andrean cult at Hexham by bringing relics of the apostle there. When he too was deposed by the Northumbrian king, he lacked his mentor's clout with the papacy and left (taking, it is thought, the relics

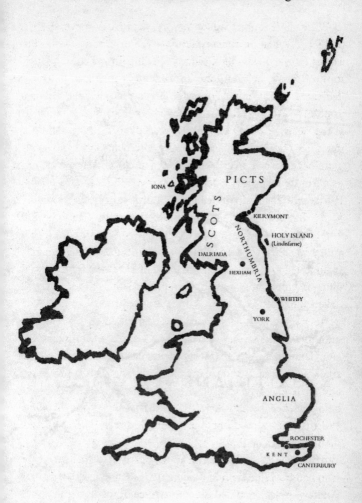

Britain in the Mid Seventh Century

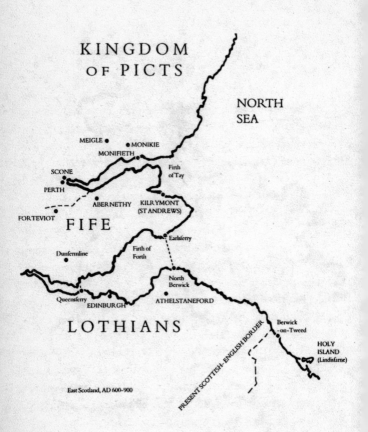

KINGDOM
OF PICTS

NORTH
SEA

MEIGLE ●
● MONIKIE
MONIFIETH

SCONE
PERTH

Firth
of Tay

ABERNETHY
KILRYMONT
(ST ANDREWS)

FORTEVIOT

FIFE

Earlsferry

Dunfermline
Firth of
Forth

North
Berwick

Queensferry
EDINBURGH
ATHELSTANEFORD

LOTHIANS

PRESENT SCOTTISH-ENGLISH BORDER

Berwick
-on-Tweed

HOLY
ISLAND
(Lindisfarne)

East Scotland, AD 600-900

with him). His natural ally would have been the king of the Picts, who had placed his kingdom under the protection of St Peter in 710.

We have now reached the point where St Andrew appears in the religious life of Scotland. The simplest, most convenient explanation for the appearance of Andrean relics in Scotland is that they were Acca's relics, sold or given for protection to the sympathetic Picts. When Acca died in 740 his body was taken back to Hexham, where he is commemorated by a fine carved cross, but his Andrean relics remained behind as the foundation of the Andrew legend in Scotland.

Various stories have arisen to explain the growth of the cult of Andrew.

As we have seen, the Picts enjoyed a somewhat wild reputation with the Romans but by the eighth century seem to have become thoroughly Christianised. King Nechtan not only voted for the Roman Church, he requested theological guidance from the Abbot of Jarrow and commissioned a church dedicated to St Peter from Jarrow architects. (The church in question is thought to have been at Restenneth, near Forfar, and part survives in the existing western tower.) Far from being a tattooed terrorist, Nechtan seems to have been genuinely pious. He abdicated in 724 to become a monk. He was succeeded in 731, after a struggle over the succession, by King Angus I (aka Angus MacFergus), who was decidedly less holy and, according to contemporary accounts, a bloody tyrant. However, he continued Nechtan's pro-Rome policy and was a patron of Lindisfarne (Holy Island), which housed the relics of St Cuthbert. The suggestion has been made that he sought to establish a similar sacred centre in his own kingdom and so brought Andrean relics to Fife.

Fife was at the centre of the Pictish kingdom. The number of villages in Fife whose names still begin with the letters Pit- are testimony enough to their origins. Fife is a treasure trove of place-name etymology, bearing the traces of Celtic, Roman and Norse conquests in its names. The one thing that is not preserved is a history of the Picts. Information about them has to be gleaned from the histories of other peoples. Their elegant standing stones show that they embraced Christianity early in history, but no one can translate them. Their language and most of their culture disappeared when they were subsumed into the kingdom of the Scots in the ninth century. This first 'union of the crowns' came about through the external threat posed by marauding Norsemen. For the Picts it proved to be as devastating as any piece of ethnic cleansing. All that remain are the silent stones, which cannot tell the secret of St Andrew's bones.

However, there are plausible reasons for making a connection between the Hexham relics and east Fife. There had been a Christian presence in east Fife since the Columban era. A friend of Columba, St Kenny or Cainnech (in Irish Gaelic), who gave his name to Kennoway in central Fife, is said to have had a hermitage at Kilrymont (another Gaelic word, which means 'the summit of the king's hill' and is sometimes spelt as Kinrymont in English). On this site St Andrews now stands.

King Nechtan had already established a bishopric at Abernethy in north-west Fife, and King Angus followed this with a monastery at Kilrymont. If he was seeking to establish something on the lines of Lindisfarne further up the coast, then Kilrymont would have been a suitable place. In the eighth century there was relative peace in the area, whereas in the ninth century Norse raids made life very hazardous for coastal monasteries, as Lindisfarne and Iona found to their cost.

Notwithstanding this, Ursula Hall makes a case that St Andrews was founded by another Angus, King Angus II, who ruled from 820 to 834 (*St Andrew and Scotland*, p. 66). The ninth century was, she argues, a more plausible setting for the establishment of a cult to Andrew. The tomb of St James had been discovered in Compostela, Spain, in 830; the bones of St Mark had arrived in Venice from Egypt in 828; and both had become the focus of patriotism and piety. And it was King Angus II who was involved in the battle of Athelstaneford in Lothian (then part of Northumbria).

The battle took place in the year 828 and gave rise to the legend of the saltire (the Scottish flag composed of a white cross on a royal-blue background). An army of Picts under Angus plus a contingent of Scots was surrounded by the Anglian army under Athelstan. 'Fearing the outcome of the encounter, Angus led prayers for deliverance and was rewarded by seeing a cloud formation of a white saltire (the diagonal cross on which St Andrew had been martyred) against a blue sky. The king vowed that if, with the saint's help, he gained victory, then Andrew would thereafter be the patron saint of Scotland. The Scots did win, and the saltire became the flag of Scotland' (from fundraising literature, Athelstaneford Flag Heritage Appeal Centre).

I prefer to believe it is Angus I who is mentioned in the legends of how St Andrews was founded and not his later namesake. There are many parallels and echoes between the Northumbrian Church and the Pictish one during the Nechtan/ Angus I era, as William Skene points out (*Celtic Scotland*, Vol. III, p. 271 ff.) – expulsion of Columban clergy, parallel churches of Peter and Andrew, chapels in honour of St Michael and St Mary. These coincidences draw us closer to the conclusion that Acca played a key role in the foundation of St Andrews/Kilrymont and that it happened in the decade beginning 730.

Yet most people in Scotland have never heard of Acca. The credit for bringing the relics of Andrew to Scotland belongs to another figure, who is surrounded by even more misty legends. His name is Regulus and he is more of an enigma than the man whose bones he allegedly brought by sea from Greece to Scotland.

When it became necessary, in the twelfth century, to explain how St Andrews became the cornerstone of Christianity in Scotland, the political situation had changed. Scotland had a new dynasty. Pictdom had disappeared. England was unified and stronger, with kings who wanted to bring Scotland under their rule. It therefore became necessary to write the story of the foundation in a way that reflected changed circumstances. In effect that meant several versions came to be written. These offer us more choice in 'How it happens that the memory of St Andrew the apostle should exist more widely in the region of the Picts, now called Scocia, than in other regions; and how it comes that so many abbacies were anciently established there, which now in many cases are by hereditary right possessed by laymen'.

That longwinded title belongs to the older of the two main legends, which is often called the Augustinian legend. In the early twelfth century Augustinian canons were imported into Scotland to 'Romanise' it all over again. Celtic practices had begun to creep back, and most monasteries had fallen into the hands of lay abbots, heads of clans whose ancestors had originally endowed them.

The legend consists of five parts and is in Latin. The first deals with Andrew's mission to the Scythian nations, where he seeks first the 'Pictones', then the Achaeans, before being crucified at Patras 'on the second day before the kalends of December'. His bones remain there until the time of Constantine's sons, when they are transferred to Constantinople until the reign of Emperor Theodosius.

The second part begins with Angus, king of the Picts, waging a cruel war against the southern part of Britain and surrounded by hostile forces on the plain of the Merse. Walking with seven companions, he sees a vision of a cross in the air and hears the voice of Andrew, who says he has come to defend and protect him provided he offers up a tenth of his inheritance to God in honour of St Andrew. With the sign of the cross preceding them into battle, Angus's troops are victorious and he duly returns to Pictdom to make his offering.

The third episode shifts back to Constantinople, where one of the custodians of Andrew's relics is fasting and praying and has a vision telling him to leave his native land and go with a guardian angel to an unknown destination. This turns out to be 'the summit of the king's mount, that is, Rigmund'.

Part four takes us back to the king of the Picts, who is sitting wearily with seven companions prior to arriving with his army at Kartenan when he is overtaken by a vision in which a man who has been blind from birth receives sight and leads the army to a place full of angels.

Part five begins: 'Regulus, therefore, a monk, a pilgrim from the city of Constantinople with the relics of St Andrew which he had brought with him, met the king at a gate which is called Matha. They saluted each other . . . and King Angus then gave that place and city to God and St Andrew the apostle that it should be the head and mother of all the churches which are in the kingdom of the Picts ... Regulus therefore, abbot and monk, with his dear companions occupied that place ... and held in his hand and power the third part of the whole of Scocia and ordained and distributed it in abbacies. This country commended itself by situation and amenities to Picts, Scots, Danes, Norse and others who arrived to ravage the island, and if they needed refuge, it offered them always a safe receptacle.'

The other main legend claims to have been copied from old books of the Picts and is more elaborate but also more fantastic. It is sometimes called the Episcopal legend, since it makes Regulus a bishop and in part one brings him home from Patras, where he fled in 345 from the army of Constantius, which was invading Patras to avenge the death of Andrew and remove his relics. Regulus, prompted by an angel, manages to rescue three fingers of the right hand, a part of an arm, a kneecap and a tooth.

Part two echoes the Augustinian version. King Angus of the Picts is facing the Saxon king, Athelstan, at the mouth of the Tyne and in a dream St Andrew promises victory and that his relics will be brought to Angus's kingdom and venerated in an honoured place. Athelstan is duly defeated and his head cut off. Meanwhile Regulus has a visitation from an angel who warns him to sail towards the north with the relics and, wherever he is shipwrecked, to erect a church in honour of St Andrew. Bishop Regulus voyages among the Greek islands for a year and a half, erecting oratories to St Andrew wherever he lands, but eventually sets sail north and on Michaelmas Eve arrives in the land of the Picts 'at a place once called Muckross ['the headland of the wild boar'] but now Kilrymont'. There he erects a cross to keep away demonic forces.

Leaving two companions to guard it, he goes north-west to Forteviot, where he meets the Pictish king's sons. Angus is away on an expedition in Argyll, and his sons pledge a tithe to God and St Andrew for his safe return. Regulus and companions (a mixture of priests, hermits from Tiber Island and virgins from Colossia) then go east to Monikie in Angus, where the Pictish queen, Finchem, is about to give birth to a daughter named Mouren. They cross the Grampians to Kindrochit, near Braemar, where King Angus meets them on triumphant return from Argyll.

The king prostrates himself before the relics and goes back with Regulus to Monikie and Forteviot, where churches are founded, followed by a grand consecration at Kilrymont, where no fewer than seven chapels are founded. Seven times they circle around, Regulus carrying the holy relics above his head, his followers chanting and the king and nobility following behind. Twelve stone crosses are erected and King Angus gives the eastern half of Fife to Regulus (i.e. a line drawn from Largo through Ceres to Naughton, west of the Tay rail bridge) as a 'parochia'. The land between the sea called Sletheuma and the sea called Ishundenema is also mentioned, which has puzzled subsequent generations. Could it be that the firths of Forth and Tay were seen as seas rather than rivers? If so, Fife would then have been the special property of Regulus and his seven churches, one of which, according to the Episcopal legend, was dedicated to Regulus himself. The document itself is attested by one 'Thana', who says he wrote it for King Ferath in Meigle.

The Episcopal legend is not without contemporary echoes. There are still a number of Pictish stones in Meigle and around Angus. Ferath figures in a list of Pictish kings *c*. 840. The monastery at Kilrymont owned lands at Forteviot and Monikie. Just south of the latter, at Monifieth, there is a church of St Rule, now a Church of Scotland building. The author clearly had access to genuine material and was not drawing local allusions out of thin air.

But how do we account for the howling inconsistencies and anachronisms? Regulus is a monk in one account and a secular bishop in another. In one story he rescues the relics, and in another he appears at the Great Gate with them. More significant, how can Regulus of the fourth century have met King Angus of the eighth century face to face? Why, if there were genuine relics of St Andrews at Kilrymont, was there no cult or attempt to do anything about this until the eighth century? Should we simply judge these legends as crude fantasies got up by later ecclesiastics at St Andrews to boost the importance of their heritage and influence? Before we brush them aside, it is worth adding a few more facts and seeing if a credible or coherent version can be pieced together.

The first fact is that there was a St Riagail, a friend of St Columba. The church he founded was at Muicinish, an island in the lake formed by the River Shannon called Lough Derg. There is no evidence he ever visited east Fife or Angus, but his saint's day is 16 October and that of Regulus is 17 October, close enough to be confused. The Irish word sounds reasonably similar to the English meaning of the Latin *regulus*, 'rule'. Muicinish means 'isle of wild boar' and Muckross, the old name for Kilrymont, means 'headland of wild boar'. Too close for coincidence? The trouble is that the sixth-century Riagail does not fit with the eighth-century Angus I (or the ninth-century Angus II, for that matter).

The second fact is that even if St Riagail did not visit Fife, there is still the presence of a Columban settlement from the sixth century. The Episcopal legend 'explains' the falling away of the thriving churches whose foundation it describes as being due to the lack of enthusiasm of subsequent rulers for the cult of St Andrew. However, after the death of Regulus (who was buried at Kilrymont) it was carried on by a group of thirteen Culdee monks who ran Kilrymont in their own eccentric manner, son succeeding father and inheriting the revenues of the monastery.

Put these two facts together and there is a case for claiming that Kilrymont had a Christian presence from the sixth century on. It was Celtic in origin (and maybe even involved the Irish Riagail in some way), but after King Nechtan's crackdown on Columban-style Christianity, it would have had to conform to Roman norms. It was also right in the middle of Pictdom and an ideal spot for Angus to found his 'New Lindisfarne' (with Acca's relics).

At this point we must introduce another candidate for the role of bone-broker. Stand up the real St Rule – or should that be the real St Rieul? Rieul was the first bishop of Senlis in France, born in the fourth century in Greece and active at Arles in Provence, then Senlis, which lies just north of Paris, near the Charles de Gaulle airport. Rieul is supposed to have died under the Diocletian persecutions, but there are a number of circumstantial links between Senlis and Scotland.

First, there was an old church of St Andrew at Senlis. Second, Simon de Senlis married Maud, King William I of England's great-niece. She founded an abbey to St Andrew at Northampton in 1084 and remarried (after Simon's death) David, who became king of Scotland. Third, in a church council in Paris in 557 the Bishop of Glasgow, St Kentigern, was present and signed himself 'Bishop of Senlis'. These connections are not highly significant in themselves but worth noting in our list of possibilities.

Third and last candidate for the role of Rule is that the name was invented and given masculine gender to convey the abstract concept of *regula*, the rule by which a monastic community might live. Or was the word *regulus* intended to indicate that the man had some kind of regal status and was not a name at all, more a title like 'kinglet'? Perhaps the truth lies in combining all these elements, as the author of the Episcopal legend may have done in an imaginative way by drawing on puns on the word *regulus*, Pictish history and the Gregory of Tours version of Andrew's life. His Augustinian counterpart, in a desire to avoid being too creative, has doggedly put down his five-part story in a way that looks clumsy and contradictory. Yet each of the five parts of his story contains a root which can be traced to other sources. The choice is not simply between a complete fabrication and a true account. It is between a mixture and a blend of legends.

One further possible explanation for the arrival of St Andrew's relics in Scotland must be mentioned. It is the simplest of all. There may have been someone who received relics from Constantinople, perhaps during the rebuilding of the Church of the Holy Apostles in 550. Maybe he decided to use the relics to convert marginal nations and went into Scythia because of the Andrew legend. He could easily have used the great rivers of Europe to travel west – the Dnieper, the Danube, the Rhine. Perhaps he came to Scotland via the Baltic – it is a more plausible journey than reaching it via the Black Sea, the Mediterranean, the Pillars of Hercules and Spain, as the other Regulus must have done. Arriving in east Fife, he then set up a cult to Andrew.

Years later Nechtan and Angus revived this cult and used it to reinforce Roman Christianity, since Andrew was the brother of Peter. The Regulus legend was constructed to bring together the two strands in the same timeframe.

I offer this as only one hypothesis among many. It is no more likely than the Regulus legend. The latter appears to have been badly treated by the Scots. We believe in the spider that taught King Robert the Bruce to 'try and try again'. We accept the portrait of Macbeth offered us by Shakespeare and turn not a hair at Mel Gibson's *Braveheart* warriors daubed in woad-coloured saltires, when we know these accounts have as much credibility as Regulus's virgins from Colossia. Yet we ignore poor Regulus, who has as much right to an honoured place in our history. Apart from the Monifieth kirk and the tower which bears his name in St Andrews (which dates from the era of Macbeth, 1040–57), St Rule is badly served.

He suffers not only from the iconoclastic backlash that occurred at the time of the Reformation and the non-existence of Pictish records but also from a revival of interest in Celtic Christianity. Rule (the non-Irish version) upstages Columba and Ninian by having got to Scotland first with his version of Christianity. Understandably, those proud of the part the Celtic Church once played in Scotland are not likely to yield the title of founder of Scots Christianity to Regulus on such flimsy historical evidence. They cannot be blamed for this, since the motives of those who wrote the Regulus legend were undoubtedly to pre-date the Celtic Church (which they only knew in days of decline), edit out the place of England in Scottish Church history (at a time of Anglo-Scottish tensions) and get back to the roots of the early Church in Greece. Just how successful they were, we shall now see.

8

A Cathedral, a Flag and a Cross

The reader who associates a 'St Andrew Cross' with St Andrew may be a little surprised to have read nothing so far about the famous X-shaped cross on which Andrew was crucified. The reason is very simple. There is no mention of such a cross in the literature or legends in the first thousand years after Andrew's martyrdom. The flag of Scotland or saltire, which features such a cross, is said to date from the battle of Athelstaneford in 832, but the legend itself comes from a later century. It also has to compete with the fact that the King Angus who had the vision of the 'St Andrew' cross in the sky is a different King Angus from the one who had the visions that are portrayed in the Augustinian and Episcopal legends. These had nothing to say about an X-shaped cross.

One was a blinding vision, similar to that of Saul (Paul) on the road to Damascus. The other was of the cross of Christ in the sky, seen by Angus and rather reminiscent of the story of how Emperor Constantine saw the *chi–rho* symbol in the sky prior to the battle of Milvian Bridge in 312 at which he triumphed and set up Christianity as the official religion of the Roman Empire. Dare one suggest that there is more than coincidence in these allusions? The writers of the legend of Angus I were trying to define a similar 'Constantinian moment' when the monarch adopted St Andrew (and the settlement at

Kilrymont). They are generally thought to be writing in the twelfth century, when King David was building up the importance of St Andrews as Scotland's answer to Canterbury; it became the nation's ecclesiastical capital in the medieval period. Both shrine and symbol played a part in bringing this about. We shall begin with the story of how the shrine on the cold, windswept promontory at Kilrymont grew into one of Europe's biggest cathedrals.

Scots history would be duller without bishops, who often played the role of bogeymen, especially after the Reformation. However, the Celtic Church, with its strongly monastic influence, was not unduly concerned about them. St Columba was not a bishop, although he kept one handy at Iona for the practical task of ordaining priests, a function which even the Celtic Church allowed to bishops. For the most part the churches of the Columban heritage operated without episcopal rule, as it was understood on the continent of Europe, right down to the time of the Culdees, who ran the Kilrymont site in the two centuries following the union of Picts and Scots under King Kenneth Macalpin in 839.

There were bishoprics of a sort. Dunkeld seems to have been chief among these sees after Columba's relics were taken there in 820. Then in the tenth century the bishop of St Andrews was made Primus – which meant he was first among equals rather than an archbishop. (It was not until 1472 that Scotland acquired an archepiscopate.)

The king who favoured Kilrymont was Constantine II (900–952), who also brought the Pict/Scot kingdom into uniformity in matters of faith and canon law. Note that it was the kings who called the shots in the Scottish Church of this era, not the

Pope. Scotland was a long way from Rome and no monarch or bishop bothered to go there (until Macbeth in the eleventh century – presumably to seek absolution for killing his rival Duncan). Constantine II himself was eccentric compared with later ideas of monarchy. His reign is said to have abounded with ale, music and good cheer. But he had an ascetic side and abdicated as king in 943 in order to become abbot at Kilrymont until his death. A cave on the north side of the tip of Fife Ness is named after him. Possibly he went there for some privacy during the festivities of ale and music!

Sources for this period of history – a thousand years in our past – are, paradoxically, sparser than for two thousand years ago. Fortunately, there are few significant developments involving St Andrew which need concern us during these two hundred years. The Kilrymont site then was certainly substantially different from what exists there today. Buildings would have consisted of timber, or wattle and daub, rather than stone. There would have been perhaps a stone church on the site of St Mary's of the Rock (today only its foundations can be glimpsed just outside the cathedral wall above the harbour).

Any threat to the contemplative life came from the Norse raiders who plundered not only Scotland and England but even France. Other, less aggressive Scandinavian immigration to France came after 911. Rollo (whose wife was Scots) went to serve King Charles the Simple, and his kinsmen, the Normans (or Northmen), settled in northern France and were to make their mark on both England and Scotland. After the Norman invasion of Britain in 1066, the entrepreneurial Normans found their way into all aspects of life, including the churches.

The happy-go-lucky independence of the Scots Church was bound to come to an end some time. The person who did most to bring Scotland in line with Roman Catholic practice throughout the rest of Europe was a woman – and a saint. Sainthood, in fact, was a family trait for St Margaret, who had several blue-blooded saints in her family tree. Her grand-uncle, St Stephen, did for Hungary what she hoped to do for Scotland – to bring it into closer conformity with the papacy and sound Roman Catholic practices. As Queen of Scotland, the indomitable Margaret was well placed to effect these reforms. Her husband, Malcolm III (Canmore, or Fathead as he was unkindly called in Gaelic), provided the brawn and she the brains as they set about persuading the Scottish clergy to be less slack in their ways – to observe the sabbath more strictly, for example, and to take communion on Easter Day. Another factor in the process was the introduction into Scotland of monastic orders that would gradually supplant the Celtic monastic system.

Malcolm had moved his seat of government to Dunfermline, in west Fife, and Margaret wished to encourage more pilgrims to visit the St Andrew shrine in east Fife. She therefore endowed a free ferry across the Forth at Queensferry. Her amazing life and character were chronicled by her confessor, Turgot, who was himself to play a part in the story of St Andrews. Turgot was a Dane who became Prior of Durham in 1087 and, after Margaret's death in 1093, was elected Bishop of St Andrews in 1107. His election brought to a head the independence of the Scottish Church.

St Margaret had relied on the power of her unremitting persuasion to make the Scots clergy reach their own accommodation with Rome. However, the Norman dynasty in England and their archbishops of Canterbury and York far preferred that the Scots should be subject to Rome through them. William the Conqueror set the tone with a demand that Scotland's churches should be subject to the Archbishop of York. He had already made Malcolm III do homage to him at Abernethy in 1072, and taken certain Lothian churches under the authority of Durham. By the time Turgot was elected bishop, the Archbishop of York was unwilling to consecrate him unless he pledged loyalty to York. Turgot gave up and went back to Durham. Malcolm's and Margaret's son, Alexander, was on the throne and decided to work a 'flanker' on York by inviting Eadmer of Canterbury to take the job. In 1120 he was consecrated a bishop by Ralph, Archbishop of Canterbury, but soon fell foul of King Alexander by stating that he was subject to Canterbury. Alexander fiercely laid it on the line that the Scottish Church was independent, but when Eadmer said he would not renounce loyalty to Canterbury for the whole Scots kingdom, it was time to go. He resigned in 1121 and went to Canterbury, where he promptly changed his mind, but was told in no uncertain terms he would not be welcome back.

These developments were central to the future of St Andrews. Had the Scottish kings played along and allowed their Church to be a province of England, the whole future of religion in Scotland would have been different and the political consequences very different indeed. Critical to the process was the combination of the next king of Scotland (David I, 1124–53) and the next bishop of St Andrews, a Norman Frenchman and Augustinian named Robert, who was Abbot of Scone. Together they cemented the foundations of a new and powerful Church centred on St Andrews.

The observant reader will notice that I have dropped references to Kilrymont. It was around the time of the 'Roman' bishopric that the old name of Celtic derivation gave way to the new name. As with many things about Andrew, no one seems exactly sure when it happened. The bishops of Kilrymont had been styled 'ardepscop Alban' since 908, when King Constantine transferred the primacy there from Abernethy. Albion was originally a Greek name for Britain and came to mean the northern part of it. Alba is still the Gaelic name for Scotland. But Gaelic was on the way out in east central Scotland, especially among the nobility, who were learning new Frenchified ways. The old Scottish kings spoke Gaelic after the Pictish language had disappeared. So did the people of Lothian, despite being part of Northumbria.

However, after the Norman conquest the people of north-east England edged north into Lothian, bringing their English tongue with them. This differed from the English spoken in the south and gradually developed into what today is known as Lallans (or Lowland) Scots. This fact irritates the exponents of Lallans as a separate language, but it also explains the affinity between Lowland Scots and their northern English neighbours. It was in this crucial period, nine hundred years ago, that French became the language of the court, which was increasingly peopled by ambitious Normans: Latin remained, as ever, the language of scholars; and 'North English' supplanted Gaelic as the common tongue of ordinary Scots. It was not surprising that in this sea change of culture and language, the name Kilrymont, with its Celtic connections, became *passé*.

We return now to the chess game being played between Scotland and England in which king and bishop (David and Robert) had significant moves to make. Before he died, King Alexander had endowed the church of St Andrew and regranted a piece of land known as the Boar's Raik to the church. Robert inherited the eye-catching church with its huge tower (108 feet high), now known as St Regulus's Tower, from which glorious views can still be had of St Andrews and all around if you have the energy to climb its narrow spiral stair. It was possibly built a century earlier to house the relics but was too small. Robert had plans, but before he could dream of a magnificent cathedral to take its place he had first to get himself consecrated.

David, equally concerned to have an autonomous Church, wrote to the Pope asking for permission to make Robert not just a bishop but an archbishop and thus make St Andrews into a metropolitan archdiocese. This would have given Scotland its own line to Rome which bypassed England, as is now the case. (An interesting modern echo of this issue came to light when Archbishop Gordon Gray of St Andrews and Edinburgh was made the first post-Reformation cardinal resident in Scotland. His mail from Rome began to arrive c/o the English Roman Catholic hierarchy until he returned it 'Not known at this address'!)

The time was not yet ripe for David and Robert. Under English pressure, the Pope declined their request. Eventually in 1124, at York, Robert was consecrated bishop by the Archbishop of York with the words 'for love of God and of worshipful King David' included, a judicious compromise in which all interests were conserved. Robert lost no time in bringing his brother Augustinians from Scone to St Andrews, where they gently but firmly began to push aside the ancient Culdees. The Augustinians in question were of French origin and were therefore 'safe' as far as upholding the line – Scottish autonomy from England – was concerned. In 1147 a papal bull gave exclusive rights to the Augustinians in the election of the bishop of St Andrews, and this gave Bishop Robert complete control of the future.

It was to include a magnificent new cathedral, around which the town would take shape, like a great arrow head pointing out to sea. North and South streets were made wide enough for great parades to and from the dominant presence of the cathedral and its precincts, which contained the busy monastery and the church tower beneath which the bones of the fisherman/apostle lay. Market street buzzed with commerce and the little harbour bustled with trade to and from the Low Countries of Europe. It was the dawn of a golden age for the little town on the king's headland. Alas for Robert, who had brought so much dynamism to his role, he did not live to see the foundations laid.

The cathedral was begun in 1160, the year after his death, first in Romanesque style and then in Gothic. It took 158 years to build, the episcopal lifetime of twelve bishops, from Robert who planned, to Arnold who founded and Lamberton who consecrated. During that time there were many quarrels, not least about the old question of English jurisdiction over the appointment of bishops. On one occasion the Archbishop of York forged a letter from the Scottish king, William (the Lyon), purporting to acknowledge his authority. On another William brushed aside the elected nominee for his own and brought down a papal interdict on the whole country. But in 1192 the matter was at last settled by a bull of Celestine III which made the Church of Scotland a 'special daughter of the Holy See', immediately dependent on the papacy and not subject to any English archbishop.

The 158 years of construction were to see a deterioration in relations with England. In many ways the cathedral began to symbolise the aspirations of the Scottish people and their different ways in matters of religion. Eventually, wars of independence fought by Wallace and then Bruce for Scotland were effectively ended by the battle of Bannockburn in 1314. Four years later, the victor of Bannockburn turned up in St Andrews on 5 July 1318 for the consecration of the great cathedral of St Andrew in the presence of seven bishops, fifteen abbots and most of the earls and knights of the realm, all of whom made offerings. The fact that Bruce had been excommunicated by a pope sympathetic to England did not worry anyone present. They had their cathedral – fought for by Scots kings, planned by French administrators and founded on the bones of St Andrew.

St Andrews was now a significant place in medieval Europe. It was to become the site of Scotland's first university in 1411 and was to play a leading role in the battle for supremacy between Catholics and Protestants in the sixteenth century. The part St Andrew took in this development changed from being that of spiritual inspiration to that of symbolic significance. The symbol which came to be associated universally with the saint, and was used on coins, seals and the nation's flag, was the 'St Andrew' cross.

The form of cross used by the Romans to crucify people was not the familiar shape we find in most of the world's churches and made immortal by some of the world's most famous painters and sculptors. The actual shape of the cross on which Jesus and others condemned to death in this way were crucified was more like a capital T. The arms were bound to the top of the T, and the legs hung down the vertical, which was firmly embedded in the ground. It is probable that the thick vertical post was left in the ground for use in other executions.

This would have been a stable structure. Not so an X-shaped cross. It would have been difficult to erect, as the cross pieces would enter the ground at an angle, and its height would have made it inclined to topple. This is amply illustrated by the painting by Preti in S. Andrea della Valle in which St Andrew is shown on his cross, propped up by extra planks and stones in order to keep him from falling over. This practical point should be enough to make us think twice that Andrew was crucified in such a way. The fact that for a thousand years after Andrew's death none of the martyrdom legends supports such a shape of cross is even more crucial.

Ursula Hall's study *St Andrew and Scotland* explores references to the cross on which Andrew died. The earliest, attributed to St Hippolytus in the third century, says that Andrew was not crucified on a cross at all but 'upright on an olive tree in Patras'. Then in the fifth century St Peter Chrysologus, Archbishop of Ravenna, states that 'St Peter died on a cross (*crux*) and St Andrew on a tree (*arbor*).' This vision is perpetuated in the bronze doors made in 1070 in Constantinople for the basilica of St Paul Without the Walls in Rome, which survive in a drawing clearly showing Andrew being attached to a tree.

The Laudatio, a text of the Acts of Andrew that dates from the ninth century, contains a passage describing the cross firmly planted in earth and Andrew looking up to Heaven, his arms spread wide to embrace the world – clearly a traditional cross. Gregory of Tours does not have the X cross, and neither do two other manuscripts that refer to Andrew's martyrdom and were widely read in the Middle Ages (the thirteenth-century *Golden Legend*, written by the Archbishop of Genoa in Latin and later printed by Caxton in English, and the tenth-century Vercelli Book, written in Anglo-Saxon).

Yet by the time of the Renaissance in many churches in Rome Andrew is portrayed with an X-shaped cross. Rochester Cathedral (an Andrean foundation from Augustine's time) altered its seal between the twelfth and fifteenth centuries so as to make the Andrew figure appear to be crucified on an X cross. The seal of Wells Cathedral (dedicated to Andrew) from 1275 shows an X-shaped cross alongside Peter's symbol. In France, as we shall see, the X-shaped cross was in use at this time. In Scotland St Andrew appears on an X-shaped cross on the Great Seal of Scotland at the end of the thirteenth century. We are driven to the conclusion that at some point – probably in the thirteenth century – the X shape was adopted and attached to the Andrew legend.

How and why did this happen? Ursula Hall quotes from *De Cruce*, the work of the Dutch scholar Lipsius. He uses for the X-shaped cross the word *decussata*, which is derived from *decussis*, the Latin name for the coin of ten asses, which has on it an X, the Roman numeral for ten. Of the X shape Lipsius states, 'Today we call it St Andrew's cross because of the strong and sufficiently old tradition that the saint was martyred on such a cross.' Unfortunately, he does not say how old it is or where he found the tradition. The X files, if we can call them that, are missing.

The earliest seal of the bishops of St Andrews to show Andrew on the cross was that of Gameline in 1255 (motto: 'Father Andrew, guide me and my rule'). Andrew, again in decussate mode, also appears on a cathedral chapter seal from the early thirteenth century. With the adoption of the saint in X shape, in 1286, on the Great Seal, the symbol of ultimate authority, St Andrew is seen for the first time as patron of the Scottish people. This was the era of conflict with England as Scotland fought to remain a separate nation.

St Andrews and its grand cathedral were by 1320 deeply rooted in the national psyche as symbols of nationhood. That was the year when the earls and barons of Scotland wrote their famous letter to the Pope asking him to urge the kings of England to let them live in peace (and independence). The patriotic language of one particular passage is oft quoted: 'For as long as one hundred of us remain alive we will never allow ourselves to fall under the dominion of the English. We do not fight for glory or wealth or honours, but for liberty, which no honest man will give up while he has his life.' For us, however, the significant point is the claim that the Scots were originally from 'Greater Scythia'. The Declaration goes on to make the connection between the Scots and St Andrew: 'Their true nobility and merits have been made plain, if not by other considerations, then by the fact that the King of Kings, the Lord Jesus Christ, after his passion and resurrection, brought them, the first of all, to his holy faith, though they lived in the furthest parts of the world, and He chose that they be so persuaded to faith by none other than the brother of the blessed Peter, the gentle Andrew, first-called of the apostles, though in rank the second or third, who he wished always to be over us as our patron.'

Here in one of the key documents of Scottish history appears the first explicit recognition of Andrew as the patron saint of Scotland. Was it simply an accident that Andrew took pride of place during the critical years of Scotland's fight for independence? Admittedly the evidence is circumstantial, but there are factors which suggest that the impetus may have been assisted by those whose native land was not Scotland but France.

When the French Augustinians began to play an influential role in Scottish Church affairs and promote the Regulus legend, it is not unreasonable to conclude that they might have been influenced by their own background.

There was considerable interest in Andrew in France. There is a legend that the church of St Victoire in Marseilles gave the cross of St Andrew to Burgundy in the first century, which, after being lost in the Crusades, was rediscovered in 1250 by a monk of St Victoire and eventually given to Patras Cathedral in 1980. In earlier centuries it had been used to strengthen the claim by the dukes of Burgundy to links with Andrew and Scythia. Their boast to have received the faith from Andrew himself was, no doubt, exaggeration but they remained promoters of the cult of Andrew. In 1429 Philip the Good, Duke of Burgundy, whose family had Andrew as its patron, had founded the Order of the Golden Fleece, with the X as its symbol.

The traffic between France and Scotland was brisk from the end of the twelfth century. There are instances of French people being sent on pilgrimage to St Andrews as penance. We have already noted connections with Senlis. Robert and the Augustinians who arrived at Scone were not the only imports from France to the Scottish Church. King David also brought artisan Cistercians from Tiron, near Chartres, to Melrose.

Put all these fragments together against a background of closer relations with France among the nobility, and we have a possible explanation of how the St Andrew legend in Scotland acquired features such as the decussate cross, the St 'Rule', who was more Rieul than Riagail and who came from Greece not Ireland. A Frenchman who had made his home in Scotland would be unlikely to want it known that the relics of Kilrymont had come from Hexham. Why not alter the time scale slightly and make it appear they had bypassed England and come direct to Scotland? The Scots would not have seen it as a lie, since they believed the relics had come from the east in the first place. It was simply a way of cutting out Acca, the middleman.

There appears to be no clear explanation of how the decussate cross came to be used so widely, especially when it played no part in the early legends. Yet from the thirteenth century on, it came to be thought of as the St Andrew cross and developed into the saltire. One plausible explanation is contained in the foundation legend itself. The original Chi-Rho symbol ($\chi + \rho$) was a Christian logo – shorthand for Christus Redemptor. The Rho is not unlike a bishop's crozier. Put the figure of Andrew where the Rho is, at the centre of the Chi: what better way of combining Andrew the apostle with Christ and recalling the Constantine legend?

To complete this circle of Franco-Scottish connections, it is worth noting that the word 'saltire' itself is of French origin – from *sauter* meaning 'to jump'.

We are not quite finished with the evolution of the legends. In 1509 William Elphinstone, Bishop of Aberdeen, produced a breviary or prayer book for the Church of Scotland 'to provide an emotional and devotional basis for national consciousness', as its purpose has been described. There is no doubt that Andrew was the central saint in Scotland at that time. Although Elphinstone's breviary was overtaken fifty years later by the Reformation and the veneration of saints generally was to disappear in Scotland for three centuries, this was yet another step in St Andrew's ascendancy as the patron of Scotland.

The Reformation had a devastating effect on the magnificent St Andrews cathedral which had for so long been a focus for national and spiritual aspirations. Its windswept shell is all that remains. The building itself was not vandalised, as many believe, but allowed to decay through neglect. However, the images of saints were torn out of the churches in the town during a whirlwind preaching tour by John Knox in 1559, and the relics of Andrew disappeared in the wave of iconoclasm. No one knows what became of them and few physical signs of the legend remain. The tower of the church which once contained the relics still stands – renamed St Regulus's Tower in later years.

For relics of Andrew we have to look to more modern imports: in St James's Roman Catholic church on the Scores a St Andrew reliquary with a fragment of bone given to the church in 1950 by the cathedral in Amalfi, and another fragment of bone from Amalfi in St Mary's Roman Catholic Cathedral at the top of Leith Walk, Edinburgh, which Pope Paul VI gifted in 1968. They provide an echo of past glories, but for most Scots the spirit of Andrew is now a much more diffuse concept.

9

Picking Over the Bones

The destruction of the cult and the cathedral did not destroy Andrew's status as patron saint of Scotland, but it resulted in profound changes in the way in which ordinary people viewed St Andrew. There was a steady evolution from piety to patriotism, from the veneration of bones to a more social and convivial use of Andrew.

In patriotic terms, for his role in securing victory at Athelstaneford, Andrew was now part of the national flag of Scotland. He also became patron of the Order of the Thistle, the ancient order of chivalry which ranks as one of the highest in the world. Founded in its present form by James V in 1540, it was revived by James VII and II in 1687, then by Queen Anne in 1703 and is now limited to sixteen peers plus royal princes. It was paralleled in Russia by the Order of Chivalry created by the Tsars which features a white X cross on blue background, also the flag of the Imperial Russian Navy.

When Scots emigrated throughout the British Empire they took their patron saint with them and founded St Andrew's societies, which began as charitable bodies for poor relief but which today fulfil a more cultural and social role. The oldest is possibly Boston (1657); then Philadelphia (1749); New York State (1756) and Baltimore (1806). The Canadian St Andrew's societies at Montreal and Toronto were founded in 1835 and 1836.

St Andrews is now the Royal and Ancient Burgh, the Auld Grey Toun, the capital of golf or the Red Gown University, depending on your priorities. It is no longer the hub of religious activity in Scotland. Even the bishops of St Andrews – and there are two – no longer live there. When the Roman Catholic hierarchy was restored in 1874 the more practical place of residence for the Archbishop of St Andrews and Edinburgh was in the latter. The Bishop of St Andrews in the Scottish Episcopal Church (who combines Dunkeld and Dunblane in his title) lives in Perth. (One of his predecessors during the Covenanter period, Archbishop Sharp, was murdered on his way through Fife, but there is no reason to suppose the change of venue has anything to do with this fact.)

Churches dedicated to St Andrew in Scotland are scarcer than one might have expected. There are Roman Catholic cathedrals dedicated to St Andrew in Glasgow and Dundee, but fewer than fifty Church of Scotland parishes out of 1,400 have the national saint in their title. Many of these are not pre-Reformation parishes, and they tend to cluster in the central and southern parts. The northern isles and north-west Scotland possess scarcely any.

One cluster of commemorations to Andrew within the presbyterian Church of Scotland is in the part of Scotland that was once Northumbrian: Dirleton, Gullane, Melville (Lasswade), Peebles and Eccles. Lothian was a staging post in the pilgrimage route to St Andrews and in Kirk Green, North Berwick, a mould was found for the manufacture of pilgrim badges. The pilgrims passing this way did not need to go further west along the Forth to the Queensferry (set up by Queen Margaret) but could cross by ferry to Fife, landing at Earlsferry.

Picking Over the Bones

As I write this in south-west France, a jet has just passed overhead in the cloudless blue sky on its way to Toulouse. Its vapour trail intersects with another which passed towards Barcelona half an hour ago. Together they form a perfect 'St Andrew' cross – a white X on a royal-blue background. I am not suggesting this is an omen, more a parable. It illustrates how the world has changed since the time of Andrew. His fellow fishermen would never have dreamt of jet aircraft – to them the silver metal bird would have seemed supernatural. The difficulty that they would have in coming to terms with our world is paralleled with the difficulty we have in coming to terms with theirs. The miracle legends of the Acts of Andrew seem hard to swallow today. We prefer natural explanations for signs in the sky, such as vapour trails or cloud formations, to divine intervention. We prefer saints who fight for political justice or feed the hungry, and thus some saints have gone out of fashion. Yet Andrew has not. One reason is that he has proved to be a man for all seasons, reinvented as occasion has demanded.

Looking back on the stages in the life (or lives) of Andrew covered by this book, I would summarise them as follows:

(1) The Jewish fisherman from Galilee, who was one of the inner group of Jesus's disciples. A strong, silent type, he was content to play second fiddle to his more volatile brother, Peter.

(2) The evangelist, first around the Black Sea coast, then in Scythia, who was martyred for his faith in Patras (or Scythia if you prefer the older but less developed version of his life).

(3) The apostle about whom legends and miracle stories were told to illustrate and promote particular theological teaching.

(4) The traveller in Eastern Europe who sowed the seeds for Christianity in Russia in years to come.

(5) The patriarch who legitimised the antiquity of an early bishop in Byzantium.

(6) The dry bones which were distributed and venerated throughout the Roman Catholic Church in Western Europe.

(7) The patron of a Pictish king who inspired a cathedral and became the patron saint of Scotland.

(8) The symbol, whose cross became a universal motif for ever linked with his name.

Not all the eight lives were legitimately connected with Andrew, but they have become inseparable from his name. That is not to debase him from a place of honour in the Christian Church. Whether or not he visited a place, whether or not they were actually his bones that were being venerated, whether or not he actually performed some of the Acts which were attributed to him matters in one sense, but it does not matter in another.

It matters for the sake of intellectual integrity, historical accuracy and sheer curiosity. On the other hand, as long as we remain honest about what is actually known, if we use legends and symbols and relics to promote faith which is grounded in reality, then it ceases to matter whether the details of the legend are factual or not. I am relaxed about the legends of Andrew. I neither want to expurgate them nor swallow them whole.

In the *Daily Telegraph*'s 'Meditation' of 20 January 1996, the Rev. Dr Denis Duncan calls Andrew an 'encourager'. Expanding on the incidents in John's Gospel in which he brings the inquisitive Greeks to Jesus and is the first to respond among his fellow fishermen, Dr Duncan puts Andrew's ability to encourage others to find faith as the prime quality for which he 'so simply yet profoundly stands'.

To be an encourager, or enabler, requires humility in order to undertake the search for faith with someone in a way which does not imply we already know it all. It also requires a strength of faith of our own if we are to guide people through confusion and not simply get lost ourselves. Those qualities of humility and strength taken together are what comes through all the different lives of Andrew. The signatories of the 1320 Arbroath Declaration of Independence – men of the sword ready to fight to the death – recognised them as important when they brought the 'gentle Andrew' into their plea.

There is another life which Andrew is living in our own times. Andrew's ninth life is to symbolise the quality of enabling and encouraging others and is still relevant today. We could no doubt reinvent Andrew the fisherman as the patron saint of our seas, which are threatened with pollution and are over-fished. Topical, relevant and legitimate as that would be, it would limit him to our own age. Better still to see him as a timeless symbol – the fisherman whose rod is the proclamation of the Gospel, whose hook is the strength of faith and whose line is the memory of what happened in Galilee at the time of Christ. That analogy is not mine but belongs to St John Chrysostom (Greek for 'Goldenmouth') in a homily on Andrew. He asks the rhetorical question 'Do dead fishermen catch live people?' Andrew might be an enigma but he retains the ability to catch the imagination of people around the world, to encourage and enable them to experience the Christian faith. In that sense, he is not dead, simply enjoying yet another life.

Select Bibliography

Cross, S. H., trans. and ed., *The Russian Primary Chronicle* (1953)

Dvornik, F., *The Idea of Apostolicity in Byzantium and the Legend of the Apostle Andrew* (1958)

Elliot, J. K. (ed.), *The Apocryphal New Testament* (1993)

Hall, U., *St Andrew and Scotland* (1995)

Hannay, R. K., *St Andrew of Scotland* (1934)

Peterson, P., *Andrew, Brother of Simon Peter* (1958)

Ross, P., *St Andrew: the Disciple, the Missionary, the Patron Saint* (1886)

Skene, W. F., *Celtic Scotland*, 3 vols. (1877, new edn 1971)

Young, D., *St Andrews* (1969)